⤙⤚ Also by Glenn Beck ⤙⤚

Broke: The Plan to Restore Our Trust, Truth and Treasure

The Overton Window

Idiots Unplugged: Truth for Those Who Care to Listen
(audiobook)

The Christmas Sweater: A Picture Book

Arguing with Idiots:
How to Stop Small Minds and Big Government

Glenn Beck's Common Sense: The Case Against an
Out-of-Control Government, Inspired by Thomas Paine

America's March to Socialism:
Why We're One Step Closer to Giant Missile Parades (audiobook)

The Christmas Sweater

An Inconvenient Book:
Real Solutions to the World's Biggest Problems

The Real America:
Early Writings from the Heart and Heartland

The
7

SEVEN WONDERS THAT
WILL CHANGE YOUR LIFE

Glenn Beck
and
Keith Ablow, M.D.

Threshold Editions — Mercury Radio Arts
New York London Toronto Sydney

GLENN:

To Tania, the woman who saved my life,
and to all those who struggle just to make it through the day

KEITH:

To my wife, Debbie, my children, Devin and Cole,
and all those who have trusted me enough to invite me
into their life stories

www.glennbeck.com/the7

Contents

The

7

GLENN

A Personal Note

I *originally intended to write something* in this space that would talk about all of the triumphs and setbacks I experienced during my journey to becoming the person I now am. But, as I started to write, the words rang hollow. I began to wonder about how honestly I could really assess myself. Would I be too critical or too easy? Could I really give an impartial analysis of how I'd changed over the years or would I be tainted by the way I interpreted my own past?

Then I had a thought: Why not ask my best friend and on-air partner, Pat Gray, a guy who's known the real me for longer than I have, to write the introduction instead? I knew Pat could write from the perspective of someone who has seen me at my highest and lowest and who has witnessed firsthand the changes I've made and the struggles I still face.

Asking Pat to write the introduction seemed like the best way for readers to see the real me now, before diving into the book and seeing what it took to get here.

Fortunately, Pat agreed.

THE GLENN NO ONE KNOWS
BY PAT GRAY

Almost no one other than Keith Ablow has ever bothered to talk to me when they're writing a story about my best friend, Glenn Beck. And that's pretty odd. After all, I've known Glenn for over 20 years, through good times and bad, both personally and professionally. Many people might think that the context I could provide would prove helpful to anyone writing about him.

Reporters apparently think otherwise. Before this book, I had been interviewed a grand total of one time about Glenn. It was a few years ago when I was still working in Houston. A reporter doing a story for a well-known newspaper called, seemingly eager to know the real Glenn Beck.

I spent 45 minutes on the phone with him, but his story only used one sentence of mine. And, of course, he tried to spin and twist the one quote he chose into something that would seem unfavorable toward Glenn. It turns out he wasn't interested in knowing the real Glenn Beck after all; he was interested in creating his own version of Glenn.

Have you noticed that the people who write stories or books about Glenn (and there have been quite a few of them) almost never interview anybody who currently works with him? It's always someone from his distant past with an axe to grind who gets quoted.

Why?

Is it that those of us who know him best have no credibility, but the guy who did the afternoon drive radio show in New Haven, Connecticut in 1993 is a 100 percent trustworthy source for all your Glenn Beck information? I don't think so. Is it that reporters can't figure out how to get a hold of me, or Stu, or any one of the other people who work here? No, I don't think it's that, either.

Sadly, I think the reason is that most of these reporters and people from Glenn's past have no real interest in writing about Glenn as a person, they care only about the controversy.

So I thought this would be a good opportunity to show them what they are missing. Let's start with Glenn's company, Mercury Radio Arts. It now employs over 40 people and has lost maybe two or three employees in eight years. There is almost zero turnover. When people come to work here, they stay here. If Glenn were the monster that so many have alleged, wouldn't there be a ton of turnover at his company? Who wants to work for a mean, hateful, racist, crazy employer?

Why is it that no one has bothered to ask how the people at Mercury can help produce three to five books a year, a live three-hour radio show, an hour of daily TV, a monthly magazine, several highly successful websites, numerous live stage tours and speaking events each year, and more? The answer is that Mercury is a well-oiled machine of people who truly care about and love not only what they do . . . but the man they do it for. Despite the intensity of the subject matter, the pressure of deadlines, and long hours, there is a fun and creative atmosphere at Mercury. The opportunities seem to be unlimited, and the possibilities seem endless. That tone is set directly by Glenn.

During the health care debate much was made about very expensive health plans that came to be known as

"Cadillac" plans. We have those plans at Mercury—and they are free to employees. Glenn picks up the full tab. In fact, our health care plan is the best that money can buy in New York State. It's not a "Cadillac" plan, it's a "Bentley" plan. And you know how many employers in New York offer this plan free to their staff? One. Mercury Radio Arts.

Mercury is a family and, because of that, we can do things that businesses with 200 or more employees could only dream of. There is no controversy, no drama, no in-fighting. And that is exactly why no one ever cares to ask about it.

It's really unfortunate because the real story about Glenn is so much more interesting than the lies. The real story revolves around a man who was very unhappy in his life—miserable, in fact—but who became extremely happy and successful by changing his life. (Yes, I know it may seem like a contradiction because of how concerned Glenn is about the plight of the country, but, believe me, while he may drive everyone around him insane, he's actually quite happy.)

Everyone can see the visible, tangible trappings of the success that Glenn has attained: *Time, Forbes,* the *New York Times,* and many others have written extensively about that. Those trappings include, of course, a multi-million-dollar company (he pays his staff extraordinarily well, in addition to the aforementioned health benefits), luxury cars, a beautiful home, and amazing vacations. More important, he has a lovely wife, Tania, with whom he has two beautiful young children, and two more amazing adult daughters. In other words, both in the material and emotional sense, Glenn has built a great life.

What most people don't necessarily see, however, is the real story of Glenn's transformation from someone who, for the most part, did not like people at all when I first met him, to a man who now genuinely loves and cares for them. From his friends and family, to his employees, business partners, and even people he's never met, Glenn's devotion is second to none.

Next time you meet Glenn out on the road at an event or a book signing, pay close attention to how he acts. Is he different when the cameras and microphones are off? Does he change when he knows that the national media isn't watching? Of course not. He stops and talks to everyone—he shakes hands and takes pictures with fans, police officers, event security, event organizers, stage hands, janitors, everyone. Again, none of it forced, stilted, or mandated by some corporate public relations person—it's completely genuine.

He also gives. He gives of his time, his voice, and his money. In fact, he often gets into trouble with the person who manages his money because he gives so much.

He has used his success to improve the lives of countless others. He doesn't share that with the world or use it as a public relations strategy; he just does it because it's what he believes in. I'm only sharing this much with you now because it's an important part of understanding his transformation; a huge part of why he is happy today. He serves others and, through that, he serves himself. He truly believes that the more you give the more you receive. And he doesn't just preach it—he lives it.

Glenn has gone from a man whose motto 20 years ago was, "I hate people" to the person, as I just described, that people love to work for. He truly engages and embraces his fellow man. We get thousands and thousands of cards, letters, notes, books, manifestos, and scraps of paper stapled to toilet tissue with a plan to save the country scrawled in crayon from fans wherever we go, and he goes through virtually all of it.

I don't mean to create the impression that we're dealing with a perfect being here. Far from it. Glenn would be the first to tell you that, like all of us, he's a work in progress. He still struggles to be a good husband and father nearly every day. He struggles to find balance in his life, and he still struggles with all the day to day pressures and distractions that most of us do.

But it is so frustrating to see those who intensely dislike him try to label him as an "actor," as someone who is insincere and says what he does for the money. Nothing could be further from the truth. No one is more sincere, no one loses more sleep, no one spends more time praying for, and worrying about, the state of the union, and trying to figure out how to wake people up to the situation we face than Glenn does. Believe me, there are far easier ways to make money if that was all he cared about.

One of the things you learn in talk radio is that you can't fake it and still be successful. (Well, I guess you can for a little while, but, eventually, you'll be found out.) With three hours on the air each day, listeners and viewers can spot a phony from a mile away. Glenn didn't become successful in broadcasting by being fake.

Back in our Top 40 FM morning-show days together, when he did fake things, and lied a lot, his success was temporary. He made a lot, and he spent a lot. It worked for a while, it brought him some fleeting gratification, but then it all evaporated. Only once Glenn opened up and became honest, genuine, and real . . . and combined it all with something you'll read about later in the book, his faith, did the windows of Heaven open up for him.

One of the biggest shows on TV right now is a reality show called, "The Biggest Loser." It follows the progress of people who are trying hard to shed massive amounts of weight. It's amazing to see people lose 100, 200, or even 300 pounds. But what's even more amazing than losing a lot of weight is when the contestants can keep it off. Many, if not most people who lose weight gain it all back within a few months. Therefore, it's noteworthy, and gives hope to others, when someone becomes so committed that they change their habits for the rest of their life. Everyone wants to know how they did it, what their "secret" was.

That's what this book is about. Glenn lost about 300 pounds of nastiness, sorrow, sin, ego, addiction, and misery in his life. But, much more incredibly, he's kept all that weight off of his shoulders for a long, long time. How did he do it?

That's the story you're about to read.

Pat Gray
New York City, 2011

The How, Why, and Way of This Book

T*his book did not happen* by accident. It was *meant* to happen.

It all began about five years ago when Glenn and I sat down together to tape a segment of his television show. We had never met before. We had never even spoken or exchanged emails. The television producers—who turn out to have known us pretty well—simply thought we would have something interesting to say to one another about the power unleashed when a person finds his or her inner truth. They had a feeling the discussion would make for a good television segment. That's all.

As the cameras rolled, we began talking about finding the courage to live honestly and fully. But we didn't stay with generalities for long. It was odd, but we felt safe with one another, as if we'd known each other for years instead of minutes. Very quickly we began talking from the heart about the wrenching challenges Glenn had faced in his life: his mother's suicide, his addictions to alcohol and cocaine, getting fired, financial ruin, health issues, and divorce.

There were the times in Glenn's life when ego or anger or greed had led him to make bad decisions that nearly destroyed him.

Many people never feel comfortable talking about such issues with one another, yet here we were, discussing them on national television, just minutes after meeting.

We talked about the fact that Glenn's willingness, after a long struggle, to admit his shortcomings and face the sources of them had been essential to his triumphs and to his pursuit of genuine happiness. We agreed that tapping into a higher power was the single most important ingredient in his rebirth and that it was the essential and ultimate key to personal transformation for every single human being on the planet.

Maybe that kind of quick trip from surface to soul is inevitable when a man who has practiced psychiatry for a few decades and a man who has triumphed over decades of deep despair sit down together—but my experience tells me that it's not. Had either of us been unwilling to really *speak* to the other, or if either of us had been intent on not really *listening* to the other, then our immediate bond would never have been forged.

That single meeting could have been our last. But it wasn't. Not even close. Such is the power of the truth.

Sharing what we really believed, if only for ten or twelve minutes on set, had forged a rare connection between us that would not be easily broken. The fact that we understood one another at a basic, human level and suspected we could trust one another felt like the start of a journey. We had no map where it would lead and no expectation that it would lead anywhere in particular. We were simply willing to believe (though sometimes that is not simple at all) that a path might already exist, that our intuitions were pointing the way to real possibilities just waiting for us to explore them. We were willing to believe we had met *for a reason.*

Everything happens for a reason.

We ended up talking many more times on television and on Glenn's radio program, speaking privately in Glenn's studio, and meeting for dozens of hours in our offices and homes. We became more than host and guest, or even just valued colleagues. We came to believe that remarkable—even miraculous—changes are possible when gifts like intuition, spirit, and intention are unlocked and embraced. We came to see that the principles that have guided my career are the same ones that have instinctively guided Glenn to replace nearly unbearable pain with genuine happiness and wonderful success.

There is immeasurable, life-altering power in these principles; they just have to be utilized in the right way.

The book you now hold in your hands is the first step toward learning how to do just that. Glenn and I are committed to sharing what we have learned about unlocking human potential. It may be the single biggest reason we met. We don't know. We'll just have to *see*. That's the point. Our eyes will have to stay open as to what might be next. And we're okay with that.

We understand that no person's life is precisely like any other's, but we also understand that one life story can reflect the challenges each and every one of us faces in attempting to love ourselves and others and pursue happiness. Mark Twain reportedly once said that "history doesn't repeat itself, but it does rhyme." The same can be said for human experiences. No two human experiences repeat themselves exactly, but there are underlying patterns that occur again and again—patterns we can learn a tremendous amount from. Why is that? Why can one life, honestly told, influence many lives? Why can human beings learn from the experiences, thoughts, and feelings of others? What energy is being tapped when one person is willing to completely open his or her heart and soul to others?

We believe we know the answer: The energy that is unleashed is directly related to human empathy—the inexplicable web of humanity that connects us all. Human empathy, while not found on any chart of human anatomy, is the reason we instinctively hurt for our children. It is the reason we can put ourselves "in the place of others" and do right by them. It powers the charity that relieves the suffering of people whom donors have never laid eyes upon, and it is the reason that one human being's intensely personal tests and triumphs can be harnessed to the good of countless others.

That is the way of this book.

So many of us believe we are alone in our shortcomings and fears and challenges and questions and hopes and dreams that we must keep ourselves undercover, lest we be seen for the imperfect people we are. But nothing could be further from the truth. There is far more that connects us than separates us. We are all struggling. We are all on difficult, sometimes tortuous, journeys that are really meant—designed, in fact, by God—to lead us to the best in ourselves.

Put simply:

"You are the temple of God." (Corinthians 3:16)

In the pages that follow, Glenn and I quote leaders and thinkers of virtually every faith and movement, from ancient times to modern times. Some of these people we'd likely vehemently disagree with on political or religious issues—but healing is not about politics, it's about understanding our place, our path, and our potential.

Our goal has been to search out the timeless, ultimate wonders of truth that can change lives. In looking for them, we searched where lines of truth emanating from many different directions intersect. We tried to show no favoritism and no fear of its source, for it is at those intersections where the ultimate light may be found.

You'll see this light manifest itself in many ways, but the extraordinary windows into Glenn's personal life may well resonate the most. We offer them not to simply show what a man is capable of, but because we know that they will rhyme with your own life experiences.

The life-changing moments of epiphany that marked Glenn's path to personal fulfillment are the same ones that therapists around the world strive for with their patients.

If you are honest with yourself and open-minded enough to accept that there are powers at work beyond those that we can document in medical journals, then you might just find that your first life-changing moment has already occurred. Glenn and I have come to realize that writing this book together at this time in our lives was no accident. Neither, perhaps, is the fact that you are now reading it.

Keith Ablow, M.D.
Newburyport, MA, 2011

GLENN

My Darkest Moment

I*t was 1996. Christmas Eve.* My first wife and I had divorced a few months earlier and I'd spent part of the day with my amazing daughters, then five and eight years old.

I remember them being so excited for Christmas that they were literally trembling with anticipation. Their eyes sparkled. They couldn't wait to wake up the next morning, find their gifts under the tree, and check whether Santa and his reindeer had helped themselves to the treats they'd left out for them. (It wasn't until much later in life that they realized their father liked baked goods far more than Santa did.)

I hoped there was enough magic in the air to blunt the hurt that was emanating from every iota of my being. When you are newly divorced and are forced to walk away from the kids you love, you know a brand of suffering that you would willingly trade for a freshly broken limb. You can't help but think you're letting them down, because you seem to be turning your back on people who love you infinitely more than you deserve.

Now, with night falling, the kids were back with their mother and I was once again alone. I looked around my place—a temporary apartment in Hamden, Connecticut. Olive green shag carpeting. Someone else's framed posters on the walls. My empty luggage stacked in a corner of the living room. It was the stereotypical sad, stale, unwelcoming, divorced man's apartment—less a home than a constant reminder of my own failure as a husband, father, and man. My children were the only beings on earth who could brighten the apartment up. When they left, I felt it. The place went from feeling like a home to feeling like a cheap, extended-stay motel room.

Luckily, the visits from my daughters were legally mandated.

It was Christmas Eve, and I was alone. No, worse than that—I was alone even though, just minutes away, there were people who wanted to be with me. That's a kind of pain that's hard to live with.

I wondered what my kids might be up to. I remembered how good it had felt when I'd been able to tuck them in and wake up with them on Christmas morning. How their smiles and laugher could light up the whole house. Then the questioning and self-doubt began: Why hadn't I been able to put my marriage back together? Why hadn't I been able to stop drinking and using drugs? Why had I worked so hard for so long and yet now sat in an apartment alone, more miserable than ever? Why could I never seem to make the right decision? Why couldn't I find real meaning in life? Why couldn't I answer the questions that continually nagged me both consciously and unconsciously? Why couldn't I interest my wife in finding any of those answers together? Why was everything seemingly falling apart?

I felt broken, and the pieces didn't seem to fit together in any way I could bear to live with. I doubted I had anything inside me truly worth loving. And I certainly didn't feel like I had anything inside me that would do anyone any good, including myself. I felt poisoned—but I also felt poisonous. I really believed if you came in contact with me, you couldn't help but become sick yourself.

Maybe you've been at that place in life and know what I'm talking about. Maybe you think you might be headed there. Or maybe you're there right now. No matter your situation, please just keep reading, because I can very much relate to and understand what you are likely going through—how dark and hopeless you might feel; how it seems like there is no way out, no way to ever find the happiness that has slipped through your fingers.

There was a time several years earlier when I was clinically depressed. I lived in Louisville, Kentucky, at the time and would drive by a highway bridge abutment on my way to work every day. In my mind, that hunk of concrete had my name on it. Often, as I approached it I would step on the accelerator. A couple of times I had even veered toward it. But I always drove right by. I could never take that final step. I was too much of a coward. It's funny, but sometimes God's blessings come in unexpected packages.

Don't get me wrong. I wanted to do it. I *wanted* to die back then. Really and truly, I did. You can feel so trapped by depression that suicide seems like a logical way out. The illness hijacks your brain. You wrongly believe—with all your heart—that death is the only answer, the only way to make everything okay again. Fortunately, a friend of mine took me to see a doctor who started me on medication. In the days before the medicine began to work I was holding on by a thread. I understood then, probably for the first time, how my mother must have felt; how she had suffered.

My mother struggled with alcohol and drugs when I was a child. My parents eventually divorced and then, when I was thirteen, my mother killed herself. I had gone to visit her in the funeral home and had to wade through all the what-ifs. What if I had talked to her more that day? What if I had been there more for her that month? What if I had listened more to her that year? What if I had been a better son?

My mother was unfailingly kind to me. She treated me as if I was her favorite, the brightest spot in her life, and she had unknowingly sparked my love for (and eventual career in) broadcasting.

When I turned eight, she gave me a collection of comedy and drama productions from the 1930s and '40s called *The Golden Years of Radio*. I became mesmerized by how the words on those albums created pictures in my mind.

Everything I had become was, in part, because of my mother, and I had never been able to get over losing her that way. It had tied me up in so many emotional knots that I had no idea how to get free.

I certainly don't blame my shortcomings on her suicide. At least not anymore. I understand that I was the one who had made a mess of my life back then, nobody else. I alone made the series of decisions that had brought me to the brink of suicide. My mother killing herself didn't mean I *had* to fall into the abyss. I chose to let that happen.

I spent decades of my life disconnected from faith and denying that free will exists in this world. I saw my circumstances as something thrust upon me, rather than the result of my own choices. I now realize those beliefs were simply the next in a very long line of misguided assumptions.

There not only is such a thing as free will in the world, but it exists even when it seems to be invisible. It crosses traditional lines of belief. My faith calls it *agency*. My father's granola-hippie–New Age spirituality (which I actually really agree with) simply said, "Life is a series of choices." Either way, free will could have been my lifeline—if only I had believed it existed.

But I'm getting ahead of myself. Before I discovered free will I had to live with the haunting memories of my mother's death. It was agony. I blamed pretty much everything wrong in my life on her suicide. My terrible decisions, I told myself, were the result of *her* terrible decision. It felt like things were on autopilot; there were no decisions to be made—I would just get up, let bad things happen, go to bed, and repeat the cycle.

I was constantly searching for an escape from my own sadness, moving from one job to another. One possession to another. One drug to another. From thirteen, to twenty, to thirty years old, I hadn't been able to think of myself as lovable because I figured that if I hadn't been valuable enough to my own mother then what could my life possibly be worth?

Even though I found a doctor to medicate my depression and keep me from crashing my car, I continued killing myself slowly by drinking myself to death.

I remember one day my doctor had looked at my blood test results and asked me what I'd been "putting into my body." I'd told him that I'd been having a drink or two a night. Technically I was right; it was only two drinks a day . . . it's just that those two drinks were gigantic tumblers of Jack Daniel's with a splash of Coke.

But the extent of my drinking wasn't the only thing I was delusional about. I had convinced myself that drinking during the day would be a bad sign. (That should give you a glimpse inside the mind of an alcoholic.) To me, it wasn't the destruction of my family, my marriage, and my liver that were the bad signs—it was the time of day that I did it. Solid logic, I know. My days had become a horror show of anxiety. I watched the clock, waiting for 5 P.M. with the focus of a sixth grader waiting for the Friday school bell to ring. I felt horrible about my life, but if I could just wait until five, then, well, I couldn't be an alcoholic, because alcoholics drink during the day.

(I should mention that I found a work-around to the

whole staring-at-the-clock thing: afternoon naps. I would intentionally go to sleep after the radio show so that the wait for five o'clock would be more bearable. If only I had thought to apply that kind of ingenuity to my personal life . . .)

I had tried to quit drinking again and again, to no avail. The lame excuses I came up with to justify my drinking didn't do much to prop up my self-esteem. That's where real self-loathing seeped into my soul. I knew I was failing to take control of my life. I knew I was acting pathetic and weak—and I hated myself for it.

I now know that millions of people experience exactly what I did. Whether they're trying to quit alcohol, stop overeating, end an addiction to pornography, or stop gambling compulsively, the feelings of helplessness are similar. I know how painful it is to feel reprehensible when you are defeated by addiction again and again. But I also know that even dozens of defeats don't mean that you can't ultimately be victorious.

Anyway, my doctor didn't seem particularly impressed with my efforts at alcohol-induced justification, either. I remember how he nodded, glanced back down at my liver function tests, and then looked straight into my eyes. "Keep poisoning your body the way you are, Glenn, and you'll be dead inside of six months. Do you understand?"

"I get it," I lied.

"I'm not kidding about this and I'm not guessing at it, either. I know what I'm talking about. I've done this work a long time."

"I understand," I said solemnly.

That night I poured myself two tumblers of Jack, with a splash of Coke in each one. I did the same thing the next night and the next. Absolutely nothing changed about my drinking—other than emptying bottles a little more quickly than I had before.

Fear could not motivate me to quit. After all, if you're not scared of dying, what are you scared of? Self-loathing couldn't make me quit. The only thing that could motivate me, I realized much later, was love.

The story I'm about to tell you isn't one that I'm particularly proud of. It's a story I tell because it's the kind of thing I once would have kept bottled up inside me (pun intended). It's a page of my life history I was once desperate to forget. That's why it's so critical to remember.

By the way, I have learned that self-disclosure is one of the best antidotes to self-hatred that you will ever find. And it's also one of the best ways to reach out to anyone who feels alone with their suffering. When you finally forgive yourself for being fallible and fragile—for being *human*—you can start forging ahead. Not until then.

God's love is there for us each and every day, but it's easy to walk right by it. In fact, as long you keep hiding parts of yourself, it's basically assured that you'll walk by it. Think about it as though you have a physical disease; you cannot be healed unless and until you are willing to *allow* yourself to be healed. Covering up your symptoms only results in your ailments getting worse. To cure them you have to stop hiding them and then go see a doctor. It's the same with healing our minds. Hiding our issues (or self-medicating them) only ensures that God's healing love is not yet welcome.

With that in mind, let's get back to the story.

The morning in question started out like any other. I woke up, got dressed, and started downstairs from my bedroom. My daughters were already up having breakfast. They heard my footsteps and ran to intercept me as I was heading toward the kitchen.

"Daddy, Daddy, tell us the story about Inky, Blinky, and Stinky you told us last night! That was the best one *ever*!"

I smiled, but inside I was confused. "Last night's bedtime story?"

"Yes! Please!"

I started to worry. I remembered Inky, Blinky, and Stinky well enough; they were the three mice I had told the girls about before they went to bed nearly every night. I'd usually create a new adventure about their mission to reach the Island of Parmesan Cheese while always on the run from Thomas the Cat. Telling them these stories was a point of pride for me as a father. I was creative, I was entertaining, and like my pasta sauce, I always found a way to work parmesan cheese in. This was something that I was good at, and it was the one time of each day that I felt successful.

The trouble on this particular morning was that I didn't remember making up a story about the mice the night before. Worse, I didn't remember reading to the girls at all. In fact, I didn't even remember being *at home*.

I had blacked out. Now, I realize that every college freshman who has done something idiotic while drunk makes that same excuse. But this was real. I hadn't deleted a horrible mistake in an after-the-fact effort at self-preservation, I had erased an invaluable memory with my daughters. Blackouts were, unfortunately, becoming a regular occurrence for me. Both at home . . . and at work.

Keep in mind that, at this point in my life, I'd convinced myself that alcohol made me a better dad. Yeah, that's right: Jack + Coke = SuperDad. That's how delusional I was. But, in my warped mind, alcohol made me more calm. More creative. It made my Inky, Blinky, and Stinky stories even better! Yeah, right.

I tried to hide my panic.

"Daddy! C'mon!"

"Tell us!"

I am ashamed to tell you what I did next, but it's the truth: I gathered my wits about me and tricked my precious daughters. Or, to put it another way, I lied to them.

"Well," I said, "if you liked the story so much, let's just see how much of it *you* can tell *me*. Were you really listening?"

Oh, yes, they had definitely been listening. They excitedly told me all about the most recent adventure of Inky, Blinky, and Stinky. (And it was pretty darn good, if I do say so myself.) I nodded at every twist and turn, pretending to remember every single word, though the reality was that I didn't recall even a single one.

That Sunday I went to an AA meeting in the basement of a church in Cheshire, Connecticut, and introduced myself. "Hi," I said. "My name is Glenn. I think I'm an alcoholic." I finally admitted that I was out of control. Lost. I didn't know how to save myself. I was powerless over alcohol.

A lot of people would end the chapter there, as though standing up at that meeting were like taking an antibiotic for an infection. But that wasn't the end of the story. Not even close. I struggled for years to win the battle I finally started fighting in that church basement. I'm still fighting it today. When the president of the United States is mentioning you by name as an example of what is wrong with America, it's hard not to start daydreaming about the deliciousness of Jack Daniel's with a splash of Coke.

I realize now that raising my hand and admitting my addiction was the end of the beginning of my struggles, not the beginning of the end. Every day is a challenge, and anyone who tells you different is probably lying. To anyone who can't understand addiction, think about it in terms of a diet. Anyone can lose some weight for some time—but how many people can keep those twenty pounds off forever? How many people can make the decision each and every day, at each and every meal, to eat healthy and go to the gym?

That day I stopped drinking, and to this day, I haven't started up again. It may sound cliché, but to anyone who has seen the darkest that life has to offer, every day in the sunshine really does count.

But sobriety was only part of it. The pain inside me hadn't stopped when I said goodbye to Jack Daniel's and drugs. And taking antidepressant medication may have lifted my mood, but it didn't do anything to get at the roots of my depression: the cauldron of toxic thoughts and feelings, stored away for so long, which were still poisoning me. In fact, two years later, I felt that pain more than ever as I sat staring at green shag carpeting alone on Christmas Eve.

I decided to write my kids a note. It wasn't a suicide

note. It was an apology. I wanted them to know what spectacular human beings they were. I wanted them to know that I had never understood before how my inability to look at myself truthfully had kept me circling around imminent self-destruction. I wanted them to know that I understood how that must have harmed our relationship and how I could be setting them up to make the same mistakes I had.

In retrospect, I think that it was hitting that low of a point, while sober, that forced me into the next stage of recovery. When you get to the bottom, you finally realize that the only thing you really own is your good name, and I didn't have one. No one in my life believed me anymore. My word was no good. I couldn't say "I love you," and have anyone believe it. I couldn't say I wanted help and have anyone believe me. I couldn't even tell anyone that I was going to go home to kill myself and be taken seriously. I'd lied too many times about too many things to too many people.

I wrote another few pages to myself that were more of the same—a tour through the mind of a man who sees goodness everywhere around him, but none inside him.

Then I lay down on the carpet and began to cry. I hurt so much. And I was convinced I had hurt too many people. Not just myself, my wife, or my kids, but other people, too—people who didn't deserve to be hurt.

Take, for instance, a coworker of mine in the early 1990s. My friend Pat Gray and I were cohosting a Top 40 FM morning radio show in Baltimore. We were paid pretty well to show up at local businesses, like car dealerships, where we'd shake hands with customers and sign autographs. One of our producers was responsible for making everything flow correctly, including keeping the line for autographs organized and moving.

One day this producer handed me a ballpoint pen to start signing autographs. I looked at it in disbelief. "I told you to bring me a Sharpie. I always use a Sharpie," I said. "Next time, please bring me a Sharpie."

The next time, he once again brought me a ballpoint pen. I fired him. Just like that. Two meaningless strikes and you're out.

A few days later, Pat noticed that the producer hadn't been to work for a while and he asked me about him.

"Oh," I said. "He couldn't even remember to bring a Sharpie with him to the signings, so I fired him."

Pat looked at me with the mixture of incredulity, disappointment, anger, and empathy that he reserved for the times I really fell short. (In other words, it was a look that I'd become very familiar with.)

"What?" I said, glaring back at him. "I warned him once. I mean, how hard is it to bring a marker to a signing?"

"Wow," Pat said. "You've totally lost perspective. You don't like yourself right now, and you're taking it out on other people. And it doesn't have to be that way, Glenn. You're a much better person than you believe you are."

"Yeah, well, whatever," I said. "I still think he was in the wrong."

"I know you do," Pat said sadly.

Deep inside, I was so scared of having no real direction in life that it had to be my way or the highway. My sense of self was so fragile I had to reinforce it in every way imaginable, including wielding the little power that I had in ways that were terribly destructive to others.

Think about it: I took a man's job away for bringing me the wrong kind of pen. *I* did that. I was *that guy.* And that poor producer was far from the only one who suffered because of me.

The memories of those I'd hurt swirled through my brain as I lay on that olive green carpet. I felt so hopeless. I curled up into a fetal position and I thought to myself, *I just can't do this. I just can't go on. One way or another— even if it's by drinking myself to death—I know I'm going to die, and soon.* Maybe that moment would have marked the beginning of the end of my life. Maybe I would have headed to a package store and gotten enough rum to start down the road to oblivion, again. (It would have been a short, dead-end street.) But instead something strange happened: I thought about my ex-wife. She was standing in front of me in our garage the day it was finally clear that our divorce was really going to happen.

She looked at me in a way that combined equal measures of real compassion and intense anger. Then she burst into tears. She poked her finger into my chest. "You are not your mother!" she yelled. "You are not going to repeat the mistakes that she made. Quite frankly, if that's what you want to do, then that's what you want to do. But you are not going to do that to your children."

You are not going to do that to your children.

That Christmas Eve those words came back to me in an avalanche of emotion. I was all alone, without my good name or a voice of my own, but I could remember the resolve in hers. I could feel it. Years after they were launched, those ten words finally connected with their target. They gave me the power and the courage to go on. Just barely. But when you're where I was, *barely* is a lot. It's the whole world. I began to look at my mother in a completely different light. I realized that, for her, the thread of hope had finally snapped. It can happen. I had been so close myself so many times.

Right then and there, for the first time in my life, *I forgave her.*

I could not yet forgive myself—not even close—but in that moment, I forgave my mother. My entire perspective on her pain had turned around. I realized her suicide wasn't about me not being special enough or lovable enough or a good enough son. You can be suffering so much that you just can't see any of that.

That didn't mean the pain instantly left me. Like that first trip to AA, there was no sudden lifting of all the weight off my shoulders. In fact, I barely got up off the floor. But I did. Only now can I look back and realize that that was an accomplishment in itself.

That night I felt no different standing up than I had lying down on the carpet. I just went to bed. When I woke up the next morning, I didn't feel any different, either. And it went on that way for a long while. I was really at a loss on how to find a way to take a single step forward. I was afraid. I didn't see a path. I didn't feel like I had any choices. Free will, it seemed to me, was dead—I had no decisions to make; no alternatives to choose from.

And that's when my stubborn side, a trait that I'd fought against for years, once again rose up inside me— but, this time, for the better. If all the doors in front of me seemed to be shut, then I'd just have to build a new door.

The First Wonder: Courage

*O*ver my decades of practicing psychiatry I've real-ized that we too often mistake courage for a combination of clarity and fearlessness. We mistake it for the absence of doubt. We imagine a passerby instinctively jumping into a raging river to save a drowning stranger, soldiers resolutely taking a hill, astronauts soaring into space, or a business leader brazenly forging ahead to create a wildly successful venture that everyone around him swore would fail.

Those acts are, of course, heroic. We stand in awe of them. But, more often than not, courage is expressed when a person can't clearly see what lies ahead, is filled with fear, doubt, or both, but manages not to give in to those feelings. As Mark Twain (yes, again) once said, "Courage is resistance to fear, mastery of fear—not absence of fear."

Real courage is more like entering a dark room that might be filled with all sorts of dangers but that may also house a great fortune. It isn't that fear or worry is absent from your heart or mind. You might well be terrified. You may only be slightly more willing to go further into that room than to bolt for the door. Such is the fine line we travel, the thread we climb, when, in the face of the inevitable struggles we all face in life, we move toward the best in ourselves—*toward God*.

Our courage is tested when we pursue difficult goals, battle financial reversals, keep on looking for a decent job, tell a friend a hard truth, try to reawaken love and passion in our marriage, try to trust again after being badly hurt, try to get sober, or resolve to say what we really think, even if we have to pay a price for saying it.

Our courage is tested when we resist taking the easy way out or giving in to negative patterns that we know in our hearts will harm us, damage other people, or show disrespect to institutions, callings, or causes that we care about.

Being tested can be incredibly painful. That's why courage so often keeps company with fear and doubt. It's the force that allows you to move forward, *despite understandable fears and doubts*, one small step at a time.

This kind of courage can be exemplified by Esther, Queen of Persia in biblical times. When Esther learned of a plot by a madman named Haman to kill all the Jews in the Persian Empire, she knew the right thing to do was to alert her husband, King Ahasuerus. But the penalty for addressing the king without being summoned to see him was death—even for his wife. It was only with great struggle, after fasting for three days and relying on the unwavering support of her cousin Mordecai, that she finally sought out the king, spoke her mind, and heroically saved the Jewish nation. Her life was spared.

Esther was afraid. She was unsure. But she found the requisite courage to not be paralyzed by her fear. She barely found the strength to do the right thing, but that was enough. It is always enough.

This is the kind of courage shown by Daniel Webster, the senator from Massachusetts. In 1850, Webster joined Senator Henry Clay of Kentucky in crafting a compromise between the North and South that helped avoid premature dissolution of the Republic, perhaps giving the North critical years to prepare for the Civil War. Webster was a towering figure and the most compelling speaker of his day, but even he admitted he was tired of having no support from his colleagues in New England. There was not a single hour, he said [as quoted in *Profiles in Courage*], when he did not feel "a crushing weight of anxiety," no meal he sat down to with "an unconcerned and easy mind."

But we don't have to go to the Bible or history books to find examples of such courage. This is the same courage shown by millions of Americans who go to work day after day worried about whether their jobs are safe, but who *keep going*. This is the courage of Americans who lose their homes and feel like hiding, but keep on showing up at their kids' Little League games, cheering them on. This is the courage of women diagnosed with breast cancer who, while fearing that their own lives could end, not only help to hold their families together, but reach out to other families coping with the same illness.

It may be counterintuitive, but admitting that we are afraid and unsure actually *increases* our courage. As the great psychiatrist Carl Jung wrote:

◡◡◡

There appears to be a conscience in mankind which severely punishes the man who does not somehow and at some time, at whatever cost to his pride, cease to defend and assert himself, and instead confess himself fallible and human. Until he can do this, an

impenetrable wall shuts him out from the living ex-
perience of feeling himself a man among men. Here
we find a key to the great significance of true, unste-
reotyped confession—a significance known in all the
initiation and mystery cults of the ancient world, as
is shown by a saying from the Greek mysteries: "Give
up what thou hast, and thou will receive."

Pretty crazy, right? Not really. By sharing your truth
with others, you are empowered. I know that Glenn has
experienced this firsthand. He often talks about the fact
that he has felt stronger after allowing others insight
into the times when he was weak. There is no defeat in
admitting your fear and pain. It is, in fact, in feeling and
facing these emotions, in embracing your humanity and
vulnerability, rather than denying these qualities, that
you find genuine courage. Because you find yourself connected to all of humanity.

Courage is a gift that is often opened with trembling
hands and it can come in many different forms.

- Courage can come from knowing that you
  have already survived many of life's challenges.
  Looking down the mountain at the trials and

tribulations you have lived through won't make you dizzy; it will steady you. Spend time to reflect on the path you've already walked.

- Courage can come from knowing that every step you take as you climb out of trouble or toward triumph will tap hidden reserves of energy inside you. Those reserves of energy have been walled off in your soul, just waiting for you to declare yourself. While it may not feel like it, facing your fears will ultimately tap that energy and fill you up, not deplete you.

- Courage can come from knowing that, at any point in time, provided you stay on your feet and keep moving forward, a new path through the darkness may be illuminated. But if you lie down or give up, you won't be able to *see* that path.

Everything can begin to change for the better in a single hour, never mind a month or a year.

And don't think for a moment that you have no role in creating the path you ultimately find. Your commitment to move forward, despite adversity, is the force that actually paves the way. A patient may not be able to cure his own cancer, but by making the decision to see a doctor that patient is attempting to find a path to success.

Finding the courage inside you is finding God. And God helps clear the way for your purest and best intentions.

Were you to employ the most powerful electron microscope on the planet or the most advanced biochemical probes or the most sophisticated genetic research techniques to explore the brain and nervous system, you would never find courage. It exists as part of us, but it is not of our flesh and blood. It is an inexplicable, higher power inside us.

Courage is one of the things Albert Einstein may have been thinking about when he wrote these words:

That which is impenetrable to us really exists. Behind the secrets of nature remains something subtle, intangible and inexplicable. Veneration for this beyond anything that we can comprehend is my religion.

- Finally, courage can come from knowing that displaying it *matters*. In the long run it matters even more than whether you win or lose in any single battle. Because courage is high character, and high character is a beacon that will ultimately attract to you all that is good in the world. It defines you in the eyes of everyone you embrace and everyone you oppose. The amount of courage you show in life will be one of your greatest legacies. It will fill your children's hearts and minds and awaken in them their own capacity to overcome adversity.

As Glenn and I prepared to write these pages, we discussed the fact that in the nearly twenty years that I have been practicing psychiatry, meeting with thousands of patients, I've never heard a single one of them find fault with a parent who struggled to make ends meet or who summoned the strength to truly battle alcoholism or who stood up for an idea he or she truly believed in and was belittled or attacked for it.

What these children, now grown into adults, remember about their parents is, in fact, the willingness they witnessed in their fathers and mothers *to struggle, to battle, to stand up.* And they held inside them the lessons they learned about courage all their lives.

We all—*every single one of us*—have moments in life that call upon us to demonstrate courage, to say what we really mean and do what we really believe is the right thing to do, even when it is very, very difficult. These moments are not accidents. They are the moments when you are being tapped on the shoulder by God or Fate or Love or whatever force in the universe that speaks to you and gives your existence meaning. You are being pressed to bring the best part of your*self* to life.

The story of one of my patients (I'll call her "Helen") makes the point especially well. She was thirty-three years old when she noticed one day that her daughter Michelle's friend, a girl named Katie, age nine, had bruises on her arm and thigh. When she asked her whether she had fallen, Katie seemed reluctant to answer, then finally nodded. "Yeah, off my bike," she said.

Helen wanted to believe that. In fact, for the whole rest of that day and the next, she put out of her mind the fact that Katie had hesitated before answering the question about how she'd gotten hurt.

But the following morning Helen woke up with a bad feeling. Her gut told her that Katie hadn't gotten hurt by accident.

A big part of Helen wished that her intuition would just go away. She didn't want to raise suspicions where they weren't justified and unfairly cast blame on Katie's parents or anyone else. She didn't want to needlessly alarm her husband and drag him into a situation she might very well be misinterpreting. They hadn't been getting along lately. If he thought she was being foolish or alarmist, they might argue, and it could make matters even worse. The easy thing would've been to ignore it.

The next time Helen saw Katie at a nearby playground, she was struck by the fact that the little girl seemed to be avoiding her. Maybe it was her imagination, she told herself. Or maybe she had made the girl uncomfortable by somehow telegraphing her suspicions.

Helen felt reluctant to do anything more than smile and wave hello to Katie's mom. She stayed at the opposite side of the playground for several minutes. She felt her palms getting sweaty and her heart racing. Why was she afraid, she wondered? She thought it might make the most sense to invent an excuse to leave the park with her own daughter. But, ultimately, a voice inside her—*the voice of courage*—told her that leaving wasn't the right thing to do. It warned her that leaving would be a rejection of her best instincts and best self. So, reluctantly, she walked over to Katie's mom, a very pleasant woman named Linda.

After they exchanged news about the neighborhood and their daughters' school, Helen only felt worse. She thought Linda seemed tense.

"I am really on thin ice here," Helen thought to herself. She had only noticed some bruises on Katie. She simply had a *feeling* the girl was hiding the truth. Feelings aren't facts. She'd heard that plenty of times. Hadn't her own daughter ended up with bruises after a soccer game or a fall off the monkey bars? No one could blame her if she left well enough alone. No one would even know the difference. And what were the chances, after all, that her daughter's friend could be in any kind of danger? Slim and none. That was the stuff of made-for-TV movies and dime-store mystery novels. This was real life.

"Well, you two have a great day," Helen said to Katie's mom. She started back toward the other side of the playground. But she just couldn't keep going. She stopped. She hung her head. A big part of her didn't want to turn around. A bigger part—a *better* part—of her prevailed. She turned, walked back toward Linda, and took a deep breath. "I don't even know how to bring this up," she said quietly.

"Bring what up?" Linda asked.

Helen stayed silent.

Linda's brow furrowed. "You okay?"

"I'm fine," Helen said. "Well, I'm not fine. But it isn't about me." She paused. "I'm not making sense." It wasn't too late, she thought to herself, to turn back before taking the plunge. But she didn't. "It's about Katie."

"Katie? What about Katie?"

"Her . . . bruises," Helen whispered. She held her breath.

Linda seemed confused.

"I'm sorry, I . . ."

Linda looked away. When she looked back, she had tears in her eyes.

Helen felt her own eyes fill up. "Why don't we head over to my house and let the girls play together?" she asked.

A few seconds passed. Then Linda nodded.

Later that day, Linda put an end to her husband's physical abuse of her daughter, once and for all, by calling the police. It turns out Linda had tried everything else. Her husband had refused to talk to a psychiatrist, to talk to the family's minister, or even to talk to his own father. And he'd been brutal with his daughter more than once.

Think about the lesson of this story: a single act of courage on a playground in one town in America ultimately led one mother to feel she had enough support from another to stop running away from violence.

It's about Katie. Her . . . bruises.

Those five words changed a little girl's life, for all time. Five words.

Helen was *called upon* to say those words. She could have chosen not to, but that would have cheated her of one of her critical moments in life. It would have cheated her of being her*self.*

How powerful are the words you might speak or the

deeds you might do when you take your first or your next courageous step? What miraculous changes for the good might you set in motion?

What should that step be? It's obviously different for everyone, but most of us simply need to follow our guts. Deep down we usually know what the right decision is. But too many of the actions we take are simply attempts to divert our attention or cover up the truth. (Glenn likes to relate this to animals. When dogs sense danger or trouble, they don't second-guess it, debate it, or rationalize it—they bark. They follow their primal instincts. Sometimes humans need to do the same.)

Take some time right now to think about what your first step might be. What is your gut telling you to do? It doesn't have to be big, but it could profoundly change your life and the lives of others.

If Katie's freedom from abuse isn't testimony enough to the power of courage in the face of fear and doubt, maybe this will be: the reason Helen ended up in a psychiatrist's office in the first place was to talk about the memories of her own painful childhood that she'd kept under wraps for decades. The trauma she had lived through and tried to bury had, nonetheless, in an inexplicable and immeasurable way, connected her with Katie's suffering. Acting to save another little girl helped her to stop running from her own past and, ultimately, to help herself.

Over time, Helen's self-esteem improved. Her capacity to be emotionally intimate skyrocketed. Even her marriage ultimately benefited. By following her own instincts and using her natural connection to other humans, she benefited herself. She gave up some of her safety, and she received far more in return.

Fear and doubt are signs that you are being tested, that it is time to begin to unlock—one step, one act, one day at a time—the God-given reservoir of personal power inside you.

GLENN

Has God Forsaken Me?

I had struggled up off that carpet on Christmas Eve and had gotten myself out of bed on all of the mornings that followed it, yet I still felt as though I had nothing left inside me. I felt, for lack of a better word, empty.

Feeling this way made me want to crawl out of my skin. I felt much more burdened and panicked than sad, like I was carrying a thousand pounds on my back and was lost on the way to a very, very important destination.

Making matters worse, I didn't even know what that destination was.

My vision was no longer blurred by substances, but it was still so clouded by my past that I couldn't see anything ahead of me. We all carry baggage with us from the complicated, often painful chapters of our life stories. Getting sober didn't miraculously make my burden any lighter.

I had lost my mother and my marriage. I had lied to my children and violated their trust. I had lost good professional opportunities because of my bad attitude.

I probably described myself to people as *empty*, or *emptied out*, or *running on empty*, a few hundred times before I finally realized that it was a clue.

Empty, I finally thought. *You've said that word enough times, now listen to it. Stop and listen. Maybe, like AA, empty isn't the beginning of the end, but the end of the beginning. Maybe to create something new and pure you must first empty out the toxic mess that preceded it.*

I figured if there was poison inside me, then it had to be like a virus corrupting a computer. A virus might infect just one tiny file, but it has the power to destroy the entire machine.

Lying to yourself is no different. Ultimately, the lies corrupt you completely. The machine shuts down. Antidepressants can make you feel better, but they can't dissolve the lies. They can make your brain work better—for a while—but they can't restore your soul. You are empty.

Okay, I thought to myself. *Don't fight it anymore, just go with it.*

If you catch your computer virus early, you have a chance to simply remove it from your system. But once your computer won't even launch its operating system, you have to go further. You reformat the hard drive. You wipe it clean. You leave nothing behind that might still be "bad code" that could worm its way through all the good.

Reformat. Leave no bad code behind.

Chemotherapy for cancer patients is another good analogy. The idea is to poison the entire body, destroying even many good, healthy cells, so that all of the cancer cells are eradicated.

Well, I took this to heart and began to question *everything*. There was just no other way forward. I swore that I would no longer be what others wanted me to be or what they assumed I had become. I decided I would spend a year or five years or ten years or however long it took saying "I don't know" until I absolutely *did* know. No more lies.

A few important things—things that I believed in to my core—got rewritten onto my internal hard drive immediately. I loved my children and I knew that. Pat Gray was my best friend in the world, maybe my only true friend. I knew that, too. I was an alcoholic who should never drink or use drugs ever again. I knew that beyond a doubt.

I also made a few important determinations that would serve as guiding principles for all future decisions: My life wasn't yet done. If I was going to keep on living, it wouldn't be in misery. I believed that people were made to be happy, and I knew that I was not. That had to change.

All of those things—from the people who loved me to the truths about my addiction and misery—were the facts. Facts. Besides those few things, there wasn't much I was willing to unequivocally say.

At that point I realized that it was very possible I had built my whole persona on something faulty. No wonder I felt unstable. It's like building a home on a shaky foundation—sooner or later the whole thing is going to crumble. No wonder I felt panicked. No wonder I had felt like I needed alcohol and drugs and the petty power I wielded in my little kingdom at work. It was all necessary to quiet the voice at the back of my mind that kept whispering, "When push comes to shove, Glenn, you are a pushover, a pretender, a fraud."

That voice was right, and I was finally ready to listen to it.

I'm not going to lie to you: it's pretty scary when you

realize that, after decades on the planet, you are a stranger to yourself. That you aren't at all sure what you really believe or who you really are.

And, yes, it is difficult to resolve to answer those questions, one moment at a time, one choice at a time. But there is no other way to become authentic. There is no other way you can end up loving, or even liking, yourself. There is no other way to triumph over timidity or false bravado.

In 1787, Thomas Jefferson wrote the words that have since become one of the cornerstones of my life. You've probably heard me paraphrase them many times on television and radio:

Fix reason firmly in her seat, and call to her tribunal every fact, every opinion. Question with boldness even the existence of a God; because, if there be one, he must more approve the homage of reason, than that of blindfolded fear.

Question everything, *especially* the things you think you know about yourself. Taking Jefferson's advice, I began to read voraciously. I bought books on philosophy and religion and politics and psychology, from the best people in world history, and also the worst. I wanted to understand what made great people great, and what made evil people evil. I purchased stacks of volumes by everyone from Billy Graham, to Adolf Hitler, to Carl Sagan, to Friedrich Nietzsche, to Aristotle, to Pope John Paul II. I read *Jesus of Nazareth* by Jefferson. I read *A Course in Miracles.* I read *The Gnostic Gospels.* I read the Bible. I read so much and so widely that the cashier at the bookstore must have thought I was buying the library of a serial killer.

But it wasn't a murder spree that I was planning, it was a learning spree. I just wanted to understand everything. I wanted to question the beliefs that were closest to my core, and see where I ended up. I questioned everything except the love of my children, the trust of my best friend, and my weakness for self-medicating my problems away.

When it came to faith, I tried it all. I tested out atheism. I was agnostic for a while. But neither rang true for me.

I realized that, deep down in my soul, I believed that there really was order to the universe, that there was a God. The logical side of me just kept asking a simple question: if there is no God, then how did all this come to be? The land, the seas, the stars, oxygen, animals, trees, flowers, humans, literature, medicine, art, empathy, love. The first atom or molecule or particle of dust in space. Where did it come from? Taking God out of the equation just didn't make sense to me.

If the Big Bang started the universe, then what caused the Big Bang?

I believed there had to be a First Cause, that a Creator had to exist, that God had to be real.

I believed it, but I *knew* I believed it only after I had pushed myself as far as I could go in the other direction; after I had faced the alternatives head-on.

The third chapter of Exodus helped me start to understand how crucial it was that my focus be on finding God not just in the seas or the cosmos, but in my*self.* In that chapter, God instructs Moses to go to Pharaoh, the ruler of Egypt, and demand that the Jews be freed from bondage. Moses hesitates:

"Who am I that I should go to Pharaoh, and that I should bring the children of Israel out of Egypt?"

So He said, "I will certainly be with you. And this shall be a sign to you that I have sent you: When you have brought the people out of Egypt, you shall serve God on this mountain."

Then Moses said to God, "Indeed, when I come to the children of Israel and say to them, 'The God of your fathers has sent me to you,' and they say to me, 'What is His name?' what shall I say to them?"

And God said to Moses, "I AM THAT I AM"; and He said, "Thus you shall say to the sons of Israel, 'I AM has sent me to you.'"

I AM. Those two simple words have been translated from Hebrew as "He Who Is"; "The Self-Existent One"; and "He Who Is Ever Becoming What He Is."

If God is everything and everywhere and inside everyone, then I figured He had to be inside me, too, and *He Who Is Ever Becoming What He Is* was just not going to let me rest until I took the journey to find my pure personal truth and full potential. I would never have peace until I became what I was meant to be.

I wasn't here by accident. I was a part of God's plan and I had to respect that plan, or at least not resent it. I had to respect my*self*, as part of Him.

I started to think of God as my own father. I thought to myself, *No good dad locks you in a room without doors or windows, without absolutely everything in that room pointing to Him, pointing the way to the best in yourself. Every-*

thing in that room must be a clue—every victory and defeat and everything you believe and everything you don't.

God wanted every gift I could bring to life. He wanted me to stop throwing myself under the bus, so he had stopped me in my tracks.

My life was supposed to have meaning. I had wandered off a path that was meant for me. So I started looking for bread crumbs to find my way back home. I stopped believing that every event in my life was a coincidence, and started to look at them as opportunities to learn. Instead of thinking I was a powerless victim working against the universe, I began to interpret events in my life as clues to what I needed to do next.

One of the books I read at that time was *The Celestine Prophecy* by James Redfield. The novel is about a journey toward spiritual awakening undertaken by a man who begins to notice *synchronicity* in his life. Seeming coincidences actually turn out to have deep meaning and importance for his personal growth. In other words, they weren't coincidences at all, they were bread crumbs.

I decided to spend thirty days without dismissing any event in my life as coincidence. Literally. If the man at the gas pump next to mine asked me directions to a museum he was visiting, and I had recently read a magazine article about that very museum, I would go visit there. If a woman dialed my cell phone and hung up once, then redialed and, upon hearing my voice, apologized for dialing the wrong number, I would say, "Well, may I ask who this is?" Because maybe, just maybe, that person was *supposed* to enter my life, in that seemingly random way. If she hung up, so be it. I wasn't going to dial back. I didn't think I should have to chase bread crumbs, just pick up the ones that sort of sat still for me.

Trust me: if you just pick up the really obvious bread crumbs, you will find that you have more than enough to find your path. It will transform your life. God isn't trying to hide anything from you. He's not being coy or playing games for His own amusement. He's trying hard to show you the way.

Be that as it may, finding my path was anything but easy. There were days that seemed to have real glimmers of light, but there were lots of cloudy ones, too. There were many, many mornings when I woke up feeling no differently than I had when I first lifted myself off that green shag carpet. And there were many nights—yes, especially the time just after sunset—when I fell back into thinking that I was just a collection of the bad things I had done, and nothing more.

Pat Gray, my best friend, kept telling me that he had found answers in his religion, which happened to be Mormonism. He told me that I was a better person than I imagined and that he might have some answers if I would give him time to explain his faith. I didn't listen to him, at least not for long enough to really hear him. I thought Mormons were, well, *strange*. I even told him so.

Some friend I was, huh?

Keep in mind, by that time there had been more than a few "coincidences" that suggested I should sit down and have a long talk with Pat about his faith. My first job in radio after high school was in Seattle, Washington. The station was owned by Mormons. My next job was at a station owned by the same company in Provo, Utah, a stone's throw from Salt Lake City. Lots of Mormons. My next job was at a station in Washington, D.C., where the news guy was a Mormon. After that, another city, another radio station, another Mormon. I think I worked for just about every Mormon in the United States at one point or another.

Many years later, after a few more pit stops, I chose a new on-air radio partner for my job in Baltimore: Pat Gray. Pat and I first met at the Baltimore-Washington International Airport. I was told that we would hate each other personally, but that we'd be great on the air together. The exact opposite turned out to be true. It took a while for our on-air chemistry to develop, but we bonded within minutes. And, Pat was, of course, a Mormon.

See, the bread crumbs weren't running away from me. I just wasn't ready to pick up the ones at my feet, because I thought I didn't like the way they'd taste.

By the time Pat and I both moved to Connecticut to work together at yet another radio station, I was feeling worn-out. I had many more enemies than friends.

That move to Connecticut was a serious blow to my career. After being courted by several prominent stations in top-ten markets, we instead wound up going from market 17 to market 103. Definitely not the direction you want to be headed if your dream is to be a successful broadcaster.

In the end, though, I believe that it was all meant to be. Things happened in Connecticut that prepared the way for my personal transformation. Of course, I didn't exactly see it that way at the time.

I bought an old house that I thought I could turn into a "dream home" for my wife and me. Instead, the house turned into a metaphor for our marriage. As we remodeled our home, our marriage underwent a similarly massive renovation. Neither turned out for the better.

Meanwhile, I really believed that I could fix the things that were wrong with the radio station, so I pursued, and obtained, a managerial position in addition to the morning show I did with Pat. It all turned out to be too much for me to handle. There were too many problems—not only with the job I had taken on, but also still brewing inside of me. There was no way I could fix a radio station (or anything else, for that matter) before first fixing my-self.

I was really, really tired—yet I was sleepless. My hopes sank. My heart was heavy.

Just months after I got sober, Pat decided he needed to move on, again. But this time he would be moving on without me. He was feeling like the station in Connecticut was a bad environment for him—in part due, no doubt, to my influence. I was unwilling to leave at that point, so Pat went off to make a life and career for himself in Salt Lake City. I found a new on-air partner. In fact, I found a series of them. But I felt more alone than ever.

There were years of indecision and self-pity. The clouds were gathering. Having now lost my wife and family and the house, having lost virtually all respect at work and in the industry, with my best friend no longer around to lean on . . . *any* bright spot in the darkness was an oasis for me.

One day, a couple of years later, I was in a parking lot talking with a colleague from the radio station. A very pretty blond woman stopped on the way to her car. "Are you Glenn Beck?" she asked.

"Yes," I said.

She smiled warmly. "You're very funny," she said. Her

voice sounded kind. "Thanks for all the laughs over the years."

I felt a little relief, just for the few moments she and I had maintained eye contact. "Thank you," I said. I actually got choked up.

That's how badly I needed warmth. That's how much I needed to be reminded I wasn't pure poison.

Later that night, I told God that I just couldn't make it through many more days sober. I begged Him to put a roadblock in my way to stop me from drinking. A sign. I needed to know He was with me. I was so serious that I actually set a deadline: Six days. I promised I'd hold out for that long because God made the whole world in six days. Surely that would give him plenty of time to throw a roadblock in my path back toward addiction.

Later that week I was hosting a car giveaway for the radio station. About a hundred people had been qualified by the station to win, and I was heightening the drama by picking the *losing* tickets out of a hat one by one. When your ticket was picked, you'd come up to me, and I'd hand you a consolation prize. The owner of the last ticket in the hat—the final contestant left standing—would be the winner. Sure, it was a little bit cheesy, but this was before I found the ratings gold of endless history lessons about Woodrow Wilson and Calvin Coolidge.

After I picked out the fiftieth ticket, a woman walked

up to me. She was the same pretty blond woman who had said hello to me in the parking lot.

She handed me her losing ticket. "Thank you very much," she said. "It was a very nice time."

I smiled. "Thank you," I said. I turned to the crowd. "This woman," I announced, "just *thanked* me for losing. If that's not the way we should all be, I don't know what is."

She seemed a little embarrassed, but she handled it all very well. She left the dealership, and I finished the raffle. I let her leave. I had missed the first sign God sent. I told you, it's the bread crumbs at your feet that you're liable to walk right over.

A few days later my deadline was up. It was time for sobriety and me to once again part ways. God hadn't come through with my roadblock, so I felt justified giving up on myself and on Him. I'd been sober about two years, and I wasn't happy. Not even close. Enough was enough. How much could one man be expected to suffer? I headed to a restaurant that I knew had a nice, long bar.

I walked in and headed right to the bar. Without hesitation I told the bartender, "I'll have a Jack and Coke." Jack and Coke. Old friends together again at last. That had always been my drink. *My* drink.

"Sounds like a plan," he said with a wink.

Well, yes, it was a plan. *My* plan.

He poured it right in front of me.

My mouth watered. I reached out and picked up the glass. I lifted it toward my lips. I turned from the bar and saw the same very pretty blonde—for the third time that week. She was sitting by herself at a little table.

I looked up at God, put down my Jack and Coke, and pushed it away from me. I told you, God is not coy. He's more likely to hit you across the forehead with a two-by-four than whisper in your ear.

I walked over to the woman. "Hi," I said. "I'm Glenn Beck. I met you at—"

"Stop. I know who you are," she said. Her smile warmed the entire bar. I smiled back. I don't think I had smiled like that—really smiled, I mean, from the inside out—for a long, long time. "Would you like to have coffee with me?"

"Yes," she said. "That would be wonderful."

It was indeed wonderful. We connected, she and I. And we've stayed connected ever since. Her name is Tania Beck. I married her about two years after that fateful night.

There are no coincidences. The challenges you face in life are not accidents; they are hurdles you must clear on the path to your true self—to honor the part of you that is connected to God, that is destined for love and happiness and success.

See, I was never without God in the days before I ordered that Jack and Coke. I was never forsaken by Him. I just thought I was. I had lost sight of the best in my*self*—including my courage and my faith. I hadn't yet absorbed the lesson from John 16:32 when Jesus, contemplating his own impending death, told the apostles not to worry:

Behold, the hour is coming, indeed it has come, when you will be scattered each to his own home, and will leave Me alone. Yet I am not alone, for the Father is with Me.

My challenges didn't end the night I met Tania. But I stayed sober and stayed committed to discovering who I really was. I kept looking for bread crumbs. And I kept finding them. And slowly but surely, my life story began to unfold in unimaginable, miraculous ways.

KEITH

The Second Wonder: Faith

Glenn couldn't have known when he asked Tania to coffee that night that she would become the most important person in his life. He could have glanced at her and turned away, telling himself it was just too late to reach out to another human being, and downed that Jack and Coke. He could have told himself he was just too broken to fix. He could have felt the drink in his hand was over-due and irresistible.

But Glenn didn't do any of that. He still had enough

faith to embrace the idea that a woman with kindness in her eyes who had turned up in his life for a third time could not be a coincidence. He had enough faith to not dismiss a bread crumb or climb over the roadblock that he had demanded.

Faith is, ultimately, the belief that you are never truly empty and that your life is never—even amid adversity—without meaning, mission, and consequence. It is the certain knowledge that there is order to the universe that embraces you, just as it does everyone and everything else. There is a healing force that elevates and energizes those who keep their hearts open, even amid distress, staying committed to a journey to become what they were always meant to be.

The Bible gives us a great example of this. When God revealed Himself to Moses in the burning bush, Moses was in hiding. He had fled Egypt for a place called Midian after killing an Egyptian guard whom he had seen beating a Hebrew slave.

Moses was chosen by God to deliver the Jewish people from bondage—used by God for a great purpose—even though he had sinned by taking a life. But before he could serve God he had to *believe* that his eyes and ears and thoughts and instincts were not deceiving him. He had to believe in himself in order to believe in Him.

Here's another example: After being baptized, Jesus

wandered in the desert for forty days to prepare for his ministry on earth. There, alone and hungry, he was tempted by the Devil to abandon his faith. But, despite his suffering, Jesus continued to believe. Then, and only then, did Angels finally appear at his side.

In order to receive the gifts meant for you, you must first believe it is still possible that they may come. That's it—no more. You don't have to go find the gifts yourself. You don't need to feel confident that all will be well. You don't need to be certain that you will defeat depression or discover your creative gifts or find true love or stop drinking forever or change an unjust law or resist oppression. You just have to believe that it is *possible*—even remotely so. You need to believe that *you* are still possible.

Why should you open your mind to that thought? Simple—because you are permanently, irrevocably connected to truth. If you think that you have been forsaken, that all is lost, or that you can never attain what you dreamed of, you are wrong. Divine power is still inside you. If you move even one step in the direction of your truest and best thoughts and actions—the unique individual you really are—you will begin to align yourself with this irresistible power and unlock your God-given capacity for joy and success.

Let go of routine and your tight grip on your present

circumstances. Just take one step. Just begin the journey. *Your* journey.

Here's a metaphor: Stunt pilots, when executing the most magnificent maneuvers, must learn to put themselves in position to roll the airplane and then *let go of the controls.* Clinging to control—out of fear—ruins the perfect arc that the plane moves in under the force of gravity. Letting go so that the Laws of Nature take over is essential.

Robert Pirsig, in his book *Zen and the Art of Motorcycle Maintenance*, shares another powerful metaphor. This one is the old South Indian Monkey Trap:

❧

The trap consists of a hollowed-out coconut chained to a stake. The coconut has some rice inside which can be grabbed through a small hole. The hole is big enough so that the monkey's hand can go in, but too small for his fist with rice in it to come out. The monkey reaches in and is suddenly trapped—by nothing more than his own value rigidity. He can't revalue the rice. He cannot see that freedom without rice is more valuable than capture with it. The villagers are coming to get him and take him away. They're coming closer . . . closer! . . . now! . . .

There is a fact this monkey should know: if he opens his hand he's free. But how is he going to discover this fact? By removing the value rigidity that rates rice above freedom. How is he going to do that? Well, he should somehow try to slow down deliberately and go over ground that he has been over before and see if things he thought were important really were important and, well, stop yanking and just stare at the coconut for a while. Before long he should get a nibble from a little fact wondering if he is interested in it. He should try to understand this fact not so much in terms of his big problem as for its own sake. That problem may not be as big as he thinks it is. That fact may not be as small as he thinks it is either.

⌒∞⌒

Maybe your problems aren't as big as you think they are. Maybe if you revalue the things in your life you will begin to reassess your situation. Is a handful of rice really worth a lifetime in captivity? Of course not, but the monkey is unable to see the forest for the trees. We are often the same way.

Don't wait for a moment of epiphany when everything becomes clear and you know exactly who you are and what you must do. Your curiosity about a topic or a cause is a sacred sign, in and of itself. It is the voice inside you whispering, "This may bring me closer to my true self. This may bring out the best in me."

Start by reading a book on a topic that sincerely interests you. Or make a call to volunteer for an organization whose mission you truly feel connected to. Mentor a child or feed the poor.

If you're struggling with alcohol dependence or drug abuse, go to one Alcoholics Anonymous or Narcotics Anonymous meeting, even just for ten minutes. If you're depressed and have avoided talking about your fears and feelings, contact a minister or therapist and schedule one visit. Just be sure you visit with a minister or therapist from a religion or healing discipline you actually have affinity for, or suspect you might.

If you dread your work and think you're destined to express yourself in another way, go to the Web and search for a course that might give you insight into what might be your *chosen* field, the one that has a legitimate, undeniable claim on your heart and mind. Contact someone already in that field to get advice. Start telling a few people close to you about what you're exploring. Begin to believe that restoring yourself is not only possible, but essential.

Be careful not to let yourself be unduly discouraged by negative feedback from others. Pursuing your truth can scare people. Whether consciously or unconsciously, they may worry you will leave them if you find yourself. They may also find it painful to watch you moving along your true path while they are still lost.

You will recognize the most loving people around you, because they will be the ones who embrace you for your courage and faith rather than criticizing or shunning you.

There are consequences for burying your real thoughts and beliefs and opinions and talents and passions. Losing your true path, wandering through life as though it is a desert, is so painful that it fuels desperation, depression, addiction, physical diseases like hypertension, and shortcuts to material riches that ultimately lead only to poverty of spirit and deep despair.

Nothing less than complete authenticity is the antidote.

As my own psychiatrist, the late James Mann, once told me, "The last place you want to be is in a first-class seat on a plane going somewhere you don't really want to go."

Ride coach if you need to, or hop a bus, for that matter, but make sure you are headed on a journey you really intend to be on—the one you were meant to be on.

There is never a time when solving the *mystery of you* becomes hopeless or unimportant. Not even when you are penniless. Not even when you are denounced. Not even when you are ill. You are never too young, nor too old. Nineteen is not too soon. Ninety is not too late. There are people who are remembered for one pure thing they do in life, very near the end of their lives. One insight. One kindness. One act of courage.

Your journey through life may have been one detour after another, through very dark thickets, for very long stretches, but it can still turn out to be just a few steps away from your true path, where the sun shines brightly and the air is clear.

Take one step. Pick up one bread crumb. Today is not too soon. It may be long overdue, but it is never too late.

Don't dismiss a friend's second invitation to meet someone he thinks could be important to you, whether personally or professionally. Open the book you notice that someone left behind on the subway seat beside you. Don't assume it is meaningless if you lose your sunglasses, and they're picked up and returned to you by that very kind person you met at the gym.

Let faith and courage carry you forward.

We are meant to be happy. We are meant to strive mightily for our heartfelt goals and achieve our genuine dreams. But in order to do so, we must first become authentic. We must strip ourselves of meaningless goals, values that don't really reflect what we believe is right, and relationships that diminish us and opinions we merely parrot.

I AM THAT I AM.

We must question *with boldness* everything we thought defined us and embrace only that which truly resonates with us at a core, irreducible level.

We must remove all viruses from the hard drives of our souls and leave no bad code behind.

After all, how could anyone love us or fight for us or respond to our needs or talents if we don't love ourselves enough to find out precisely who we are and live in accordance with what we discover?

There is a path meant for each of us, and it is not only our right, but our sacred responsibility, to find and follow it. The path may be covered with leaves. Shiny trinkets or temptations may have distracted us and coaxed us away from it. Overwhelming fear may have made us run from it. But, please, please, have *faith* that the path has always been there.

Famed Scottish mountaineer and writer W. H. Murray, who served as deputy leader to Eric Shipton on the Everest Reconnaissance Expedition of 1951, put it this way:

⌒∞⌒

Concerning all acts of initiative (and creation) there is one elementary truth, the ignorance of which kills countless ideas and splendid plans: that the mo-

ment one definitely commits oneself, then providence moves, too. All sorts of things occur to help one that would not otherwise have occurred. A whole stream of events issues from the decision, raising in one's favour all manner of unforeseen incidents and meetings and material assistance which no man would have dreamed would come his way. I have learned a deep respect for one of Goethe's couplets: "Whatever you can do, or dream you can, begin it. Boldness has genius, magic, and power in it. Begin it now."

Every major religion and culture has identified faith as a force that unlocks mysterious and magnificent energy. The Book of Mormon puts it simply and directly:

. . . Whenever men have had sufficient faith, angels have ministered unto them.

Hinduism, Taoism, Chinese popular religion, Siberian shamanism, and other spiritual traditions speak of a polestar. This star, in direct line with the earth's axis of rotation, is thought of as the anchor to which the entire solar system is tied by aerial cords. It is said that the star's very rotation causes the sun, moon, and all other stars to also turn. It is the celestial engine that powers the splendor of the universe.

In ancient Vedic wisdom, the polestar is literally Dhruva—a prince who, at age seven, sought out God. Many argued he was too young for such a quest. Even when he met up with the revered Saint Narada, the saint told him he should return home. Undaunted, Dhruva coaxed Narada to teach him to meditate. He then chanted by the banks of the Yamuna River with such determination and for so long—with such *faith*—that, as it is written, he indeed met the Lord and was ultimately rewarded with his kingdom's throne.

In this sense, the entire universe, according to Vedism, can revolve around one person's inner resolve to find truth and pursue his or her destiny.

You have a polestar inside you. It is connected with all the energy in the universe. When you begin to follow that star you align yourself with immeasurable, inexplicable forces that will actually help you manifest your best intentions.

I have a friend who is a good example of this. He was hired to run a group of small clothing stores owned by a large department store chain. The stores were struggling to make a profit. He was up for the challenge and took the job.

He loved the work of building a new brand name in the retail arena, but he couldn't convince his bosses to embrace his creative impulses and bold strategic instincts. In fact, when he laid out his plan to save the stores and expand them, his employers told him they wanted "nothing to do" with such sweeping changes.

Undaunted, my friend carried on. He devoted enormous energy to trying to run the stores more profitably, even given the inherent constraints. But with his vision stymied, and his voice as a leader partly silenced, he wasn't able to create a powerful enough business.

The department store chain eventually decided to close the stores or sell them—even if it meant taking much less than they had invested in them. In their minds, the brand just hadn't caught on. My friend was exhausted and dispirited. He would be out of a job and wondered what kind of future he would have in the field he loved.

He felt so embarrassed that he decided to keep the news from his mother. She was seventy-one at the time, and he didn't want to appear weak or make her worry about him. But one night, at dinner, she told him he seemed "beaten down." She asked him how work was going.

"Work is . . . work," he said. "I'm fine."

She looked at him in that loving and insistent way she had always been able to—asking him again for the truth.

"What?" he asked.

"This is me you're talking to. You don't sound 'fine.'"

He smiled at her intuition, shook his head, and let out a long breath. "I think they're going to sell the stores or close them," he said. "They just don't see the kind of future for them that I do."

A few long moments passed.

"I'm sorry," she said. "I know how much work you put into them. I know you believed in them."

"I did. I believed in my vision for them. I just wasn't able to make it happen."

His mother nodded to herself. "You could make it happen now."

"Now? No, you don't understand. There's no time left. They're getting rid of them."

"I know that," she said. "So, what stops you from finding partners and buying them yourself?"

"*Buying* them? *Me?*"

"Weren't you frustrated they wouldn't give you what you needed to succeed?"

"Well, sure. But, listen: when push comes to shove, that's not their fault. I wasn't able to convince everyone to take the risk."

"That's not the issue now," his mother said. "The issue now is whether you can convince yourself."

"It's not that simple. Even if I could find investors, even if I could run the stores exactly the way I wanted to, nothing in life is a hundred percent. I could still fail. And then I'd have wasted a lot more time and probably a lot of money."

"It's okay to fail," she said. "Everyone fails at some point. Now, you have to ask yourself whether you're really afraid of failing or you're afraid of winning. Because if this works, it's going to test you. And you won't be able to walk away from it. Not for a long time. It would be like walking away from your child."

"I loved working on this project," he said. "And these stores do have incredible potential. I know it, for sure. But, you have to understand, to dedicate even more of my career . . ."

She reached across the table, took his hand, and looked him in the eyes. "Stop making excuses. Make good."

That conversation took place in 1998 between Julian Geiger and his mother, Mildred. That's the year when Julian assembled a team of investors and purchased a group of little stores from Federated Department Stores (now known as Macy's). Those stores are named "Aéropostale" and today there are more than one thousand of them. The company now trades on the New York Stock Exchange, employs more than thirty thousand people, and generates net profits of about $400 million a year.

When Julian recommitted to his dream and had the freedom to pursue it, his vision became contagious to everyone in his organization—from his investors, to his management team, to store managers. His personal energy and clarity of purpose triggered commitment and courage from all those around him.

I'm not surprised. The sphere of thought of our entire species and of all human behavior is ultimately engineered to support and propel the genuine gifts you bring to life.

I cannot overstate this fact. Embracing yourself by committing to your real beliefs and real goals—just one step at a time—not only means you stop swimming against the tide of your true desires; it means you are carried forth by a mighty current of truth that is always sweeping forward the most heartfelt thoughts and actions of human beings.

Remember, no matter how far you have wandered from your fullest potential as a human being, you can find your way back to it—but only if you have faith.

The Gnostic religion, an offshoot of Christianity that broke with the orthodox church during the second century A.D., speaks of the importance of *remembering who you truly are, not who you have allowed yourself to become.*

In the Book of Thomas the Contender, part of Gnostic scripture dating back about 1,600 years, it is written this way:

He who does not know himself, does not know anything, but he who knows himself, knows the depth of all things.

The Gospel of Thomas includes these passages:

. . . If you seek the Kingdom of God in the sky then the birds will precede you. And if you seek it in the sea, then the fish will precede you, but the Kingdom is in you. And if you know yourself then you know the Kingdom of God.

. . . If you bring forth what is within you, what you bring forth will save you. If you do not bring forth what is within you, what you do not bring forth will destroy you.

As you commit to unlocking and bringing forth the truth inside you, don't be afraid to pray for help. Don't be reticent to sit with yourself in silence and meditate. Connect with the miracle of spirit, of God, that has lived inside you from long before you were born. You will be rewarded, as will those lucky enough to know you or to be touched in powerful and immeasurable ways by your ideas or actions.

All things are possible through God. But you must first have the *courage* to have *faith* that He will show you the path if you let Him.

Why Can't I Just Wish It Away?

Meeting Tania for the third time in a week was a bread crumb—but I was still at the very beginning of my path. She needed to be patient with me. I was, after all, still the man who had just ordered a Jack and Coke. Not taking a sip of it didn't seem to be all that important. Like firing a bullet at someone, but missing, my intent was there, even if the result wasn't. I was guilty and, worse, I was still uncertain and unsteady. I had committed to staying on the planet and I was trying to look for my path through this life, but I was still very much lost when she found me.

It goes without saying, but you can't just wish away your pain. You must have courage and faith, and they will give you what you need to survive in terribly dark places and through terribly tough times. But you need truth to find your way into the light.

I was on the run from my truth. I was in *denial* of my truth.

I had moved every couple of years for almost my entire adult life. For decades, I blamed that on one job ending and another beginning, but I know now that I was the one who ended those jobs. It was a pattern of mine. It was no accident. It was no coincidence. Unconsciously, I was *making it happen* so that I didn't have to really see myself for the profoundly pained and flawed person I was. The pattern allowed me to forget the past, over and over again, without learning from it, dealing with it, or changing because of it. It allowed me to bury all the broken promises I made, all the times I let friends and family down, all the times I spoke loudly and forcefully and hurtfully to others and had no real knowledge to back up what I was saying. It allowed me to fool myself into thinking that I would leave alcohol and drugs and depression in the rearview mirror and start fresh because I would be hundreds or thousands of miles away, at a new radio station, surrounded by new people.

Well, guess what I learned? You can't run from your past. I'm not exactly sure why it took me so many years and so much pain to learn it, but I did. You can't really benefit from courage and faith if you haven't stopped to look deeply and honestly at your past. Why? Because your past inevitably shapes your present circumstances and defines your future. If you don't take the time to understand it, then it will consume and control you.

Moving from city to city, job to job, or relationship to relationship to escape negative influences doesn't make a whole lot of sense if *you* yourself are attracting the negative influences.

Physician and author Jon Kabat-Zinn puts it this way:

Wherever you go, there you are.

I could have gone to Europe or Tahiti or anywhere else in the world and re-created the same flawed dramas, attracted the same broken people, kept my distance from the same positive influences, and made the same lousy decisions. You can't outrun yourself, and you can't outrun your past. The lies you tell yourself, whether consciously or unconsciously, are much more corrosive than the lies you knowingly tell others.

Denial of reality—past and present—is a special kind of hell. It separates you from your best self, which is the same as separating you from God.

Denial needs lots of fuel to keep the truth at bay. Plenty of things will do for a while, even though none of them last. That includes alcohol, cocaine, expensive toys, traveling ceaselessly, working endless hours, and frantically pursuing fame. Anything that distracts the mind and soul from turning inward, where it really needs to turn.

Believe me, I've tried most everything to keep the truth from shining through. I don't know anyone who hasn't tried *something*. It is the human condition that we all fear the realities that hurt to look at the most. And it is also the human condition that we heal to the extent that we *do* look.

The late Madeleine L'Engle, author of *A Wrinkle in Time* and *The Rock That Is Higher Than I*, wrote:

∽

Truth is frightening. Pontius Pilate knew that, and washed his hands of truth when he washed his hands of Jesus. Truth is demanding. It won't let us sit comfortably. It knocks out our cozy smugness and casual

*condemnation. It makes us move. It? It? For truth
we can read Jesus. Jesus is truth. If we accept that
Jesus is truth, we accept an enormous demand: Jesus
is wholly God, and Jesus is wholly human. Dare we
believe that? If we believe in Jesus, we must.*

I didn't believe in the power of truth inside me—not at the core of my being. I had read book after book in my quest for knowledge and had many new ideas and facts in my head. I had summoned courage and faith in order to stay alive and stay sober. But I was still too afraid to honestly look at my past in an effort to learn every lesson I could.

In all fairness, how could I not be afraid to do a real self-evaluation? Running from the truth was a big part of my family's legacy—though it's clear now that sometimes you don't realize you are lying to yourself until you can see it in the rearview mirror.

When I say that, I'm not dodging any personal responsibility for my mistakes. My parents had burdens they carried through life and they did the best they could to shoulder them with the resources they had.

I love my parents deeply, but it would not honor them to *pretend* that they weren't afflicted with the same scourge of denial that nearly killed me. And it should come as no surprise that I now have a real aversion to pretending. I can spot a fake person a mile away (my friends will tell you that I can even spot a toupee across a crowded room) and I can't stand being around them.

I have learned that a complete commitment to keeping your eyes open—especially when you wish you could close them—is the only way to clear your vision and see the path that's been laid out for you.

My mother was on the run from reality, in a big way. She spent most of my childhood on drugs and alcohol, hiding her addictions from everyone she could. She had so many layers of denial that it was difficult to know what was real and what was fake anymore. It was all an illusion. My mother was lost. She never spoke of whatever it was in her early life experience that had made her so vulnerable to her demons, and I doubt she even knew, but I have tried to figure it out. So far as I can tell, my mother was sick with unrealized potential. She had grown up in the 1950s and early 1960s and had missed the whole hippie thing. She came of age just before that—when women were supposed to take care of the house and cook for the kids and keep a lid on any other goal they might have.

My mom was Martha Stewart on steroids. She was the most creative person of all time. All she wanted to do was own her own flower shop—It was her *dream*. But my grandparents would have thought that even taking one step toward doing something like that was absolutely insane. They didn't see any reason my mom needed to learn to *drive*, let alone start up a business. Ulitmately, she never did either one.

I believe that when she saw talent in her daughters she instinctively, automatically squashed it. Her self-concept was so damaged that she projected it onto them, incessantly criticizing and undermining them.

She told one of my sisters, who is blessed with extraordinary artistic talent, that she was foolish to think of herself as a painter. My mother told her that again and again, to tear her down, because my sister's talent and her intention to use it were a threat to her. She was afraid to come face-to-face with the talents she had never been allowed to express, dreams she had abandoned, goals she had never reached.

Dreams are important. They're messages from God. When you ignore them or resist them or are kept from pursuing them, you are cut to the core of your being. Inevitably you then inflict injuries on others, too.

My mother was even worse to my father. She was verbally abusive and unfaithful to him. He accepted it because he had lived through plenty of abuse much earlier in his life and was so focused on not being an abuser himself that he became the abused. He was trying so hard to not become *his father* that he was instead becoming his mother.

Like I said, running from the truth was a big part of my family's legacy.

I didn't really know at the time just how much damage my mother was doing to others, because I was the one person she was unfailingly kind to. But the idealized version of her that I held in my heart just set me up for a bigger fall when she eventually left me. I was the place on earth she had put the best of herself—the reservoir of her humanity—so I was blindsided by her suicide. I was suddenly left without a love that was, perhaps, exaggerated because it was so intensely focused on only one person—*me*.

Even if I had been prepared to grieve in any real way (which I wasn't), my father had other ideas. He responded to the loss the best way he knew how: by moving the family on from it. He meant only the best for us, and he worked two jobs to try to make a new life for the family. My stepmother, meanwhile, worked three jobs while trying to raise two teenagers she barely knew. To put it mildly, the family was busy, or at least intentionally distracted.

At thirteen, I not only buried my mother, I also buried my grief and anger over losing her and my guilt over being the singular object of her affection. Unconsciously,

I figured that it would all stay buried. I buried it so deeply that I didn't even notice the way that it led me to do everything in my power to avoid any truly intimate relationship or to really trust anyone ever again. I buried it so deeply that I didn't notice the way it fostered a knee-jerk cynicism in me toward anything good and decent. I buried it under layers of anger, guilt, and booze. I buried it so deeply that I never once confided in my first wife that my mother had committed suicide.

I stayed silent about the most traumatic event in my life because that's how I knew to deal with such things. That's how red-hot the burning embers of that memory still were for me, deep inside. I wouldn't touch them. That decision almost ended with me killing myself and hurting many people—including my children, who likely would've continued the family tradition of running from the truth.

Think about how ludicrous this really is: I thought of killing myself in order to avoid knowing myself. Does that make any sense at all? And lots of people do kill themselves, for the same reason. I'm not talking just about suicide. We drink ourselves to death. We eat so much that our bodies crumble under our own weight. We overdose on drugs. We soothe ourselves with cigarettes or other vices. And so many of us who don't face death only hobble forward in life, gambling compulsively, watching pornography obsessively, experiencing insomnia and de-pression and panic attacks.

We go through these things simply to avoid taking that hard look inside and dealing with the ugly stuff we know we'll find there.

What have you buried? Do you think the life events and memories you hide from yourself and others are uniquely shameful? *Really?* Do you think, as I did, that you are poison? Do you not see that we are all flawed? Unfortunately, the vast majority of us believe we would be shunned forever if we wore our truths pinned to our chests, but that's the biggest lie of all.

For me, the love of a woman helped turn the tide. Tania was the one who was gentle, insistent, and brave enough to make me face myself. She wouldn't settle for my evasive answers when she asked about my family of origin. In fact, she led with her own painful memories so that I wouldn't think I was alone in sharing mine. She was the one who listened to me describe what I thought was the worst poison inside me and, most important, she was the only one who wanted to hear more, so that she could better understand me.

Tania was the one who entered my life and stayed in my life when I didn't think I was worth anyone's time, let alone love. Was I lucky to find her? Was it destiny or coincidence? Was it always meant to be? The truth is that I don't really care. It doesn't matter. I was in a place where I was looking for bread crumbs. If my eyes had been closed, then it wouldn't matter what brought Tania and me to the same bar that night, because I never would have seen her.

I remember one day when I was in the kitchen and I was falling back into a pattern of self-loathing. It was a day when my demons were hovering around in clear view. I certainly wasn't in good shape financially or professionally (or physically, but that goes without saying), but, more important, I wasn't in good shape emotionally. I was searching for my truth, and it felt like those burning embers in my soul were just beneath the surface. I hurt. I hurt a lot.

I know now that it's supposed to hurt. It's supposed to hurt like the worst pain in the world. I don't know what giving birth feels like, but I imagine that this kind of pain is close. And why shouldn't it be? You are, after all, being reborn. How could I not expect to suffer as I waged war on the demons I had sheltered for a lifetime?

The truth may set you free, but as President James Garfield once said, it will first make you miserable. And that's what I was: *miserable.*

I walked up behind Tania and put my arms around her. I had to tell her she was making a terrible mistake. I knew how good she was, but I was like a black hole draining that goodness right out of her. "I just don't know why you'd want to be with someone like me," I told her, tears welling up in my eyes. "I have nothing to offer you. I am not a good person. I am stealing all of your light."

Do you know how she responded? It was such a beautiful thing that I worry that writing about it won't do it justice. But I have to try because I want you to know how love can heal. She pressed her arms over mine and said, "You cannot steal that which is being freely given." Wow. Free will, right? She could leave at any time. But she didn't—she was still right there; loving me more than I loved myself.

What happened next may not come as much of a shock to you: I cried. I cried because another human being knew me and didn't think I would infect her with whatever poison had corrupted me. I cried because she believed I was capable of redeeming myself. I cried because someone thought that I, an alcoholic loser, had something of value to offer her.

In 2008 I published a novel, *The Christmas Sweater,* which was loosely based on my life. While many of the scenes were created or exaggerated for the story, one was not: a dream I had one night that changed my life forever. In retrospect, I think it was actually more of a prompting than a dream but, either way, it woke me up at three in the morning and was so powerful that I immediately got out of bed to paint a picture of what I'd seen.

The novel has a much longer and more detailed description of what the experience was like, but here's a brief recap. I was standing in a cornfield, at the end of a road, under a gray winter sky. On each side of me were broken cornstalks. It was winter, and there was a little bit of snow, but not enough to cover up the dirt underfoot. Everything was brown and dark and dead.

Right in front of me, at the end of the roadway, was an utterly black cloud—almost velvet black. It absorbed all the light around it, and I felt it calling out to me.

I was not about to go forward toward the storm, and I didn't see any other road, so I thought to myself, *Well, I can't go through that storm, so I guess I'll have to stay right here.*

Just then, an old man in tattered clothing, with a big, grayish beard, walked up to me and whispered, "You must walk through it."

"Oh, no," I replied. "I can't. It's too big, too violent, too angry."

He whispered again, "You have to walk down this road."

I fired back, more firmly this time, "No. I can't! It will kill me."

He smiled. "Really, there's nothing to be afraid of."

"No."

"Glenn, go through it. Just take a step."

I stood there for a while, my fear palpable.

That's when he grabbed my hand and softly said, "Come with me."

Somehow, we got to the other side. I don't know exactly how. But however we ended up there, the next thing I knew I was *facing* that velvet black cloud, looking at the back of it. The road I was standing on wasn't gray and dreary anymore; it was bright and clean. Everything was lush and green and beautiful. It was like a Technicolor dreamworld. It was breathtakingly, indescribably beautiful.

"This is what awaits you on the other side of the storm," the old man told me.

I looked over at him. He had transformed. He was now dressed all in white and his hair was pure white and glowing.

"This *is* the other side," he said. "There's nothing in between. It's just the fear that stops you from going through it. It's warm and beautiful here. Walk through the storm, and all of this awaits you."

That's the last thing he said to me before I once again found myself on the other side of the storm, back with the dead cornstalks, snow, and bitter cold.

That's when I woke up. And started painting.

I still have the picture I painted that morning at 3 A.M. It sits at the back of my closet. I keep it to remind myself what the world looked like to me before I took real steps down my path.

For me, AA was the main forum I used to resurrect the pages—whole chapters, really—of my life story that I had tried to tear out and bury. I took my personal inventory and started to catalog and share all the horrible things I had been keeping inside me.

It was so important that people were willing to listen to me and ask me tough questions designed to get me thinking even more deeply than I might have by myself.

And, maybe for the first time in my life, *I* started to listen—*really* listen, to other people. I listened to my sisters tell me things about my mother that I once would have refused to believe. I listened to my father answer questions about his own suffering in life that, just months before, I would never have thought to ask him. I listened to my young daughters in supportive, open ways I never had before. I could see them with greater clarity and I felt more joy in their presence than I had ever before. It made me love them more fully than I ever knew I was capable of.

Then, one day, when I was hosting my radio show,

a caller put me on the spot. He asked me point-blank whether I had ever used drugs. I think everybody working in the studio expected me to deny it. But I had just about *had* it with denial. I knew it was the worst kind of poison. "Uh . . . yeah," I said. "*Yeah!* I have; I've done a lot of bad things."

After those words came out of my mouth, I told my producer at the time, Stu Burguiere, that he should write down the date, because it would be the date I had ended my career.

I couldn't have been more wrong. Just the opposite happened. That was the day I started doing radio that really began resonating with people, because I was telling *the truth*. My audience started to grow because listeners could trust me. I wasn't acting anymore. I was *authentic*. And ultimately, what people hunger for is authenticity— from others and from themselves.

Give it a try. Start revealing the truth about yourself and just watch whether you're ostracized or embraced. In the end, I know it will be the latter. And I also know that being embraced for anything other than your truth is a cold comfort. It isn't real. It will only keep you on the dark side of those black storm clouds.

No, I couldn't just wish my pain away. I had to stop running from it and turn and face it, even though it hurt—a lot. Then I had to learn to share it.

So do you. There is no other way forward. You must stop playing a shell game with your truths. You must get rid of the outdated software your mind has built to keep reality at bay. You must walk through your storm.

The truth will set you free, but first it will make you miserable.

The Third Wonder: Truth

T *he power of truth is* inside you, waiting for you to discover it, even if you have been running from it for a lifetime. It is never too late to turn and face the real story of how you became who you are in this world, in order to rid yourself of any emotional or behavioral patterns— especially unconscious ones—that are undermining your possibilities. You can put yourself at one with immeasurable and extraordinary forces by removing the "viruses" corrupting the software of your soul.

How can you do this? The answer is by unearthing the chapters of your life story that you once buried, thinking they were just too painful to ever reread. Those are the ones that contain runaway, misinterpreted, toxic messages and themes from childhood or young adulthood or even just a few years ago that are your sapping your potential.

Imagine if someone were to ask you to read pages 125 to 225 of a five-hundred-page novel and then write an ending in which the lead character finds tremendous success. Chances are you'd feel anxious and unprepared. You'd be coming into the story midstream, without knowing the character's motivations, strengths, and weaknesses. "This isn't my story," your heart would tell you. "How am I supposed to make it come out right?"

In order to write something credible and convincing, you'd want to know what happened to the main character in the first 124 pages. You'd want to know what writers call the character's *backstory*—his or her earlier life history. Without this information, you would likely feel that you could not move forward with confidence; that the next chapters you would write would ring untrue to readers.

When we try to move forward with our lives without a true understanding of its earlier chapters, we ask ourselves to do something that is no less fraught with difficulty.

Stop moving blindly ahead and start moving closer to your truth.

Resolving to do this work—and, make no mistake, it *is* work—requires both of the first two wonders that Glenn needed to remake himself: courage and faith. After all, you wouldn't have buried certain facts about your life if you didn't believe they had the capacity to hurt you. That's why you need courage to dig them up. And you wouldn't ever go digging at all if you didn't have the confidence that you could overcome the pain you'd been avoiding in order to evolve into the person you were meant to be. That's why you need faith.

Courage and faith pave the way to embrace the truth you have been wasting energy resisting. And when you do embrace it, you will be cleansed and transformed by it.

Think about Glenn's vivid dream. He was on one side of a velvet black cloud, standing in a barren, threatening landscape. He needed to move through that blackness to the lush, green, sunlit landscape that awaited him. The black cloud didn't capture him. He didn't remain forever amid the demons as he feared. He moved *through* them.

There is no way around digging up the painful parts of your life story, but you *will* get through that pain. And you will find a land more warm and beautiful than you can imagine on the other side.

I call this spiritual alchemy *The Pain to Power Principle*. When we finally stop denying the traumas and trials we have lived through and instead resolve to learn everything we can from them, then they are inevitably turned into the power of self-determination, self-esteem, and self-expression.

I promise you that this alchemy really does take place. Like empathy and courage, you can't *see* this particular transformation happening—you can't point to it in a book or see it in a microscope, but it's there nonetheless. From the minute you turn to look at the demons you have been trying so hard to run from, you begin to take all of their momentum away from them and harness it to your advantage.

The great poet Rainer Maria Rilke once wrote:

How could we be capable of forgetting the old myths that stand at the threshold of all mankind, myths of dragons transforming themselves at the last moment into princesses? Perhaps all dragons in our lives are really princesses just waiting to see us just once being beautiful and courageous.

Marry faith and courage with the truth, and you create something that is far more than the sum of its parts—

you unleash an energy, an extraordinary momentum that is as powerful as it is inexplicable.

Avoid the truth, and you instead invite stagnation and suffering.

If Glenn had not been willing to see how his mother's remarkable, singular love for him (and her inability to show the same love to her husband or daughters) had made losing her even more traumatic, he might have decided to keep his distance from Tania. Her capacity to love him completely might have actually driven him away, because it could have felt vaguely discomforting and threatening—unconsciously connected in his mind to a past loss, rather than to wonderful possibilities for the future. In fact, Tania's love could have triggered more drinking and self-medicating, or maybe another cross-country move—anything that would have helped him escape coming face-to-face with the painful past he had lived through and refused to revisit.

If unconditional love had forever remained linked with unbearable loss in Glenn's mind, he never could have opened himself up to it again. As a result, he would have lost out on a marital relationship that has transformed him, given him two more magnificent children, and provided a strong family foundation from which he has built a remarkable life.

If unconditional love had forever remained linked

with unbearable loss in Glenn's mind, he would have been ill-prepared to forge emotionally open, honest, unconditionally loving relationships with his two adult daughters. The flawed patterns of the past—the emotional viruses that had inhabited his soul—would have infected yet another generation. His daughters may well have chosen men to marry who reproduced the flawed ways in which they learned to relate to their flawed father. And their own children would also likely have borne the burden of the viruses.

Generation after generation would pay the price—with interest—for Glenn's unresolved emotional pain. Denial would snake its way into the future, covering its tracks and Glenn's God-given path and even obscuring the paths of his children and grandchildren.

Fortunately, it didn't happen that way. Glenn found the courage and the faith to make it happen a better way—by embracing the truth. His willingness to finally grieve his mother's death properly and wrestle with the realities of her shortcomings allowed him to properly connect his sadness and confusion and anger over her suicide with the particular circumstances of that tragedy, rather than allowing those emotions to float free and attach themselves to other relationships in his life.

In my experience, every person who has come to me for help—whether with depression or addiction or anxiety or marital difficulties or complicated grief or simply to become more empowered in life—must do the work of excavating the distressing parts of his or her life story that that person has buried. Every person must resolve to look at the very events and psychological dynamics he or she has lived through and would most like to forget.

Each and every one of us must defeat what Sigmund Freud called the "pleasure principle"—the human instinct to seek pleasure and avoid pain, including painful recollections. We must instead embrace the Pain to Power Principle—the idea that uncovering, facing, and understanding one's pain is the only way to overcome it and to find our paths to true emotional freedom and true self-expression.

Why do so many people hesitate to take this leap? It's just human nature. Many people believe that they are leaping into quicksand and that they will drown in painful memories. They believe that the truth will be overwhelming and that they will be unable to survive it.

They are wrong, of course. But that worry—of drowning in truth—fuels all the disabling ways we seek to avoid it.

We take irrational risks and then busy ourselves cleaning up the inevitable messes. We find one distracting or debilitating relationship after another. We lose weight and then gain it back again. We send thousands of text messages and emails a week in the hope of hiding from the part of ourselves we don't want to think about.

You don't have to hide. I say this unequivocally and I say it based on two decades of experience: No one drowns in the truth. Ever. And you won't, either.

Sure, there are times when it may feel overwhelming to face the truth head-on, but it ultimately buoys people and carries them downstream toward better places in life.

Of course, looking at your life story honestly and completely can trigger feelings of sadness and anxiety and anger and regret, but those emotions come along with the precious gifts of insight you are getting ready to receive. Even going on vacation requires getting your work affairs in order, packing, going to the airport to be frisked, waiting at gates through delays, and sitting in a cramped plane for hours on end. But no one would turn down a week in paradise simply because of how arduous the journey might be.

You are ready to vanquish the demons you have been fleeing. How do I know? Because you wouldn't be reading this book if you weren't. You wouldn't have picked it up, or you would have put it down quickly. It is in your hands this very moment *for a very good reason*. This is a bread crumb on your path. Do not ignore it!

I want to be very clear: Glenn and I believe with all our hearts that you were meant to be reading these very words at this very moment in your life. So, ask yourself, "Why? What am I supposed to see more clearly now?

What's happening in my life, or *should* be happening, that makes it the right time?" Think long and hard about the answers to those questions.

I know that you may be in the very earliest stages of self-discovery. I want you to know that you will make it. There are untruths in your existence that you will need to clean out, but you will get there. It may not feel like it now, but you really will.

You will also have moments in life—maybe very soon—when you will have the opportunity to make an important difference in your future, the future of people you love or, perhaps, the future of people you have never met, but to whom you are nonetheless spiritually connected. Do not let the pain of the past dominate that future. Look squarely at it, be strengthened by it, and turn it into power.

The current of energy that flows in your favor when you stop denying what you have lived through and how it has shaped you and how you must change is the immeasurable force that you can tap into to dramatically improve your existence. It is, ultimately, a force that was inside your soul from before your birth and is inside your soul this very moment. It will never leave you. You can rely on it. It is nothing less than your connection to God.

All of us have a barometer of truth inside us. The truth is what people value most highly. It's therefore no surprise that putting yourself in accord with it should put you at one with the richness of the universe itself.

Here's a different, more tangible way to think about this concept. Why would people have bid all the way up to $3 million for the record-setting baseball that St. Louis Cardinal Mark McGwire hit out of the park in 1998? That baseball represented McGwire's seventieth home run in a single season, the most home runs ever hit in one season by a major-league baseball player.

But guess what? That baseball was made of the same exact stuff as the thousands of others that are used every season. It was leather and string and cork. But those are just its physical attributes. The reality is that the McGwire baseball was so much more than the sum of its physical parts. It had a real-life story attached to it. It had real history attached to it. It symbolized a moment in time when baseball fans everywhere felt they had witnessed true greatness. That's why, at the time, it was worth a fortune. It symbolized a truth.

Today, that baseball is worth just a fraction of what the winning bidder paid. The reason is that Mark McGwire has since admitted to using steroids during 1998. His athletic achievement was a lie, a fraud. Experts have suggested that his fakery could cut the value of his home-run baseball by 90 percent. It may eventually be worth about as much as a new baseball at Kmart.

The 7

vived a divorce and *survived* alcoholism and *sur-* …ug addiction.

…ay it, again: No one drowns in the truth. Ever. …ther will you.

… of my patients, a woman I'll call Carolyn, makes …t especially well.

…olyn was forty-two years old, thin as a rail, and …exhausted when she first came to see me. She had …symptoms of major depression—sadness, tearful- …s of appetite, decreased concentration, and wak- …t four each morning.

…an't fall apart," she said, in tears. "Everyone's …g on me."

…unting on you for . . ." I asked, leaving the sen- …en for her to complete.

…y husband isn't doing well again. He has MS. I …t we had beaten it. I really did. He took time off …ork and started a new medicine. It seemed like his …ms really went away. I fooled myself into thinking …re gone forever. Now it's back, worse than ever. …ry weak. I just don't know what to do."

…ow long has your husband been ill?"

…e was diagnosed a year or so before we met. It …bad back then. He just had tingling in his arm and …t figure out why. It came and went. The worst he …d with it while we were dating was some numbness

---

There are two lessons. The first is that truth is worth more than anything you can physically see or hold. Truth is priceless, and anything that encapsulates it becomes price- less as well. The second lesson is that only complete truth stands the test of time. Anything less will eventually turn from priceless to worthless and people discover that they were deceived.

People spend vast fortunes to own original art. They want to possess it. They want to be near it. Single paint- ings by Jackson Pollock and Gustav Klimt and Vincent van Gogh have brought as much as $150 million. Why? Because we all hunger for authenticity. We want the real thing, not a copy.

Don't let yourself be a copy. Be an original.

Harry Crews, one of my favorite writers, described his own acceptance of truth so eloquently that I want to share some of it with you.

For many and complicated reasons, circumstances had collaborated to make me ashamed that I was a tenant farmer's son. As weak and warped as it is, and as difficult as it is even now to admit it, I was so humiliated by the fact that I was from the edge of the Okefenokee Swamp in the worst hookworm and rickets part of Georgia I could not bear to think of it, and worse to believe it. Everything I had written [in my rejected manuscripts] had been out of a fear and loathing for what I was and who I was. It was all out of an effort to pretend otherwise. I believe to this day, and will always believe, that in that moment I literally saved my life, because the next thought—and it was more than a thought, it was dead-solid conviction—was that all I had going for me in the world or would ever have was that swamp, all those . . . mules, all those screwworms I'd dug out of pigs and all the other beautiful and dreadful and sorry circumstances that had made me the Grit I am and will always be. Once I realized that the way I saw the world and man's conditions in it would always be exactly and inevitably shaped by everything which up to that moment had only shamed me, once I realized that, I was home free. Since that time I have found myself perpetually fascinating. It wasn't many weeks before I loved myself endlessly and profoundly. I have found no other such love anywhere in the world, nor do I expect to.

⚜

When you commit to being a true original—to stop running from your real life story and real feelings and real

dreams—you will elicit the s
ers. When you stop pretendi
mitting that you have strug
spiritual energy will fill you.
does the truth feel so threat
river that will carry me to a
like quicksand?"

The answer is that the m
ied were from times when
and easily hurt—during chil
when we suffered such jarrin
completely disempowered.
"recorded" these memories a
children, we still feel exquisit

When Glenn was in his t
rienced grief and anger over t
what he was really experienci
year-old child. It was the fea
abandoned and terribly alon
remained "frozen in time"
to the fetal position on that
Christmas Eve. The thirteen-y
have died than faced his grief.

It was only after he foun
was able to change his entire
realized that he could call on
had *survived* the loss of his m

and *sur*
vived dr
I'll
And nei
One
this poi
Care
looking
several
ness, lo
ing up
"I
countin
"Co
tence o
"M
though
from w
sympto
they w
He's ve
"H
"H
wasn't
couldn
suffere

in his hands. But that went away, too. "She smiled, but only for a moment, then shook her head and wiped away a tear. "He used to say I must be his 'antidote.' "

"He needed you—"

"He still does. Which is why I can't fall apart."

"Right."

"I have a son from a prior marriage, and we have two girls together. And I'm working as a teacher, while I'm trying to hold everything together. So I thought maybe if you had something you could prescribe . . . I mean, just to sleep, even . . ."

"A medicine might help," I allowed. "But I really want to know more about you. Your first marriage—how did it end?"

"My husband ended it," she said.

"He filed for divorce?" I asked.

"No, he overdosed and died," she said. "He was an addict."

"I'm so sorry to hear that."

"It was a long road," she said. "I met him in college. I should have known back then. I mean, the way he used drugs wasn't . . . recreational."

When a woman marries twice—each time to a man struggling with a serious illness—there's a reason. "Did you struggle with depression then, too?" I asked.

"Of course. It was a very dark time for me. I took

something that helped, though. A sleeping pill at night and an antidepressant. I don't remember the names. Maybe if you ran some of them by me . . ."

I didn't want to run by anything. I wanted to linger long enough with Carolyn's pain for her to *stop* running. "Was that the first time you had been that depressed?"

"No. Well, *yes.* I mean, it was the first time in a long, long time." She seemed a little irritated. "That isn't the issue, though. The issue is that I'm struggling *now.* I need to sleep. I have to have enough energy to get things done at home and keep my job."

Carolyn seemed to be working hard to avoid sharing the history of her episodes of depression. "I understand," I said. "I really do. It just helps me to know whether the depression is entirely new or not."

"Okay . . ."

"When you say you got depressed during your first marriage for the 'first time in a long, long time,' I take it you had been depressed many years before that—at least once?"

"I mean, that's ancient history. I'm talking, when I was a kid. I don't even know if it was depression. I just remember being out of it in, like, the fifth grade. I just felt very weak and very sad. I couldn't concentrate. And I remember I cried a lot."

"Had anything happened to make you so sad?"

"Sure. It wasn't out of the blue. My best friend back then, Lauren, got leukemia." She stopped, suddenly choked up. She cleared her throat. "She, uh . . . was really amazing going through it." Another tear started down her cheek. She fell silent.

Several moments passed.

"I'm sure she showed a lot of courage," I said.

"She was incredible. But there was nothing anyone could do. That's what my mother said, 'There's nothing the doctors can do.'"

"You miss her."

The tears really started to flow. Carolyn wiped them away, then literally looked at them on her fingertips. "What is this? I didn't come here to talk about Lauren."

I knew, of course, that Carolyn *had* come to talk about Lauren—at least in part. The death of her childhood friend seemed connected to so many later chapters in her life story. She had married two men who were ill. She had partly defined her role in their lives as the one who could keep them healthy. When she was unable to do so for her first husband, she became depressed. Now, unable to "cure" her second husband, she was depressed again.

"I wonder if you really believe there was nothing anyone could do," I said.

More tears. "She didn't deserve what happened to her."

"Nobody deserves leukemia, Carolyn. At least she had a friend like you in her corner."

She shrugged.

"You know, it takes a lot of strength to stand by someone who's suffering the way Lauren must have been."

Carolyn looked directly at me. "I wish to God I could have done more."

"I know you do," I said. "I bet Lauren knew that, too. I bet it meant the world to her." I paused. "You can love someone very much and not be able to cure them of an illness. It can make you feel powerless, when that isn't the case at all."

She smiled bravely. "I think I know that. Maybe I don't really believe it, though."

Carolyn *didn't* believe it. Deep down, she believed—with the heart of a bereaved child—that enough love should cure leukemia or drug dependence or multiple sclerosis. That's why she had spent so much of her life running away from the fact that tragedies can strike the people we are closest to without notice and with dire consequences, even when we *do* love them, even when we do our best to keep them safe and sustain them. It probably explained why she tried to heal two husbands and fell victim to major depression each time that she wasn't able to. It probably explained why, as I learned over the course of several more meetings, she had used so much of her energy trying to track every symptom of her husband's multiple sclerosis, to research every possible remedy, and to convince him to visit specialist after specialist, all around the country.

Carolyn was so intent on defeating her husband's disease, in fact, and so terrified that she would ultimately be unable to, that she had never allowed herself to ask him how he *felt* as he struggled against it. She had never let him take the lead and be supportive *of her*. And she had never given her children permission to vent their feelings about their dad's challenges. Her fear that she had failed her childhood friend Lauren had short-circuited powerful psychological forces that could have strengthened her bond with her husband, made her family more cohesive, and given her children the example of expressing their feelings rather than stifling them.

Once Carolyn was able to *see* all this, she was able to overcome her depression by sharing and *feeling* the sadness and anger she had been running from. She began to take joy in the fact that her husband was himself motivated to overcome his symptoms. Suddenly, she was much more aware of his remaining, substantial strengths than the weakness in his muscles. She ultimately used some of her energy to pursue an additional degree in education, rather than to scour the Web for new therapies or schedule consultations with neurologists in other states. Her children were able to watch their mother and father *living life*, rather than fearing death.

This is the way that truth works in the real world. It frees us from ingrained, negative, self-limiting patterns to which we cling out of fear. It frees our children, and their children.

It is never too late to embrace your truth. It doesn't lose its charge like a battery. It doesn't age as we age. It remains at its full, miraculous strength, waiting for you to discover it.

The Buddhist teacher Sogyal Rinpoche (I told you we'd be looking far and wide for inspiration!), author of *The Tibetan Book of Living and Dying*, wrote:

❧

Saints and mystics throughout history have adorned their realizations with different names and given them different faces and interpretations, but what they are all fundamentally experiencing is the essential nature of the mind. Christians and Jews call it "God"; Hindus call it "the Self," "Shiva," "Brahman," and "Vishnu"; Sufi mystics name it "the Hidden Essence"; and Buddhists call it "buddha nature." At the heart of all religions is the certainty

*that there is a fundamental truth, and that this life
is a sacred opportunity to evolve and realize it.*

❧

How can you begin to do this? Some people go to psychotherapists. Others go to pastoral counselors. Others begin to meditate. Still others start with twelve-step programs like Alcoholics Anonymous or Al-Anon.

Whatever works for you is what you should do, but we've developed a four-step plan to help you get under way.

STEP ONE:

*Show Courage and Faith by Beginning to Put Down the
Shield You Have Been Holding Up to Keep the Truth at Bay*

What do I mean by a "shield"? It's any habit you've gotten into to distract yourself from thinking and feeling. Shields include things like drinking too much alcohol or using illicit drugs or eating to excess or smoking or playing the lottery compulsively or working ceaselessly or losing yourself in one dramatic, romantic relationship after another.

Any shield you carry only gets heavier with each passing day. It steals your energy and focus and cheats you of seeing that you are strong and full of potential. And it keeps others from seeing your strength and potential, too. As long as you're holding up a shield (or more than one), you're living in fear, and people sense it.

Imagine that just beyond the shield is a mirror capable of reflecting who you are and how you became that way, going all the way back to your earliest years. You can't see yourself in the mirror because the shield is in the way. But you *need* to see into it because it will reveal the painful thoughts and feelings you've been running from. Only then will you start to realize that you have been fleeing the very things that can make you authentic and connect you with all the energy that flows in the direction of truth.

You don't have to quit drinking completely to begin putting down your shield. You don't have to get in perfect physical shape. You don't have to stop working every overtime shift. You don't have to be a monk. You just have to start lowering a shield (or maybe a few of them)— even just a tiny bit, so you can peek into that mirror and let a little of God's light reflect on you.

The truth has its own inherent force. Open the door a crack, and the truth will make a visit—maybe only bringing a moment of clarity, perhaps a brief recollection of a bit of your life experience you've avoided thinking about for years or decades.

Then, just open the door a little more, and then, even a little more. Keep going, even when it hurts.

Every kind of growth in the world requires confronting pain. You can't strengthen your muscles in a gym if you're not willing to hurt the next day. You can't recover from an injury that affects a weight-bearing joint unless you're willing to do the necessary rehabilitation and walk through the unavoidable discomfort. You can't bring life into this world if you're paralyzed and terrified by the birth process.

Your spiritual rebirth is no different.

I don't want to minimize the effort involved. It takes courage and it takes faith to lower shields, especially when doing so starts to reveal emotions and memories you've been avoiding. You'll have to keep reminding yourself that you deserve to find your true path. You'll have to keep an eye on the irrational fear of truth that can make you think of it like quicksand instead of the crystal-clear, moving, purifying current it really is.

If you put your shield down partway, then end up raising it again, please don't give up. Remember, it may take trying again and again before you can finally keep the shield down for good.

STEP TWO:

Identify Emotional or Behavioral Patterns in Your Life That You Want to Change

Maybe you always find yourself romantically involved with overly dependent men or women. Maybe you always end up in conflict with female colleagues old enough to be your mother. Perhaps you find yourself setting up new business opportunities, and then backing out at the last minute. Or maybe you can't seem to ever leave a situation, even when you really should.

Most of us have at least one such pattern and can identify it pretty quickly. If you aren't aware what yours is, ask a few trusted friends or relatives who know you well. You might say something like "I'm trying to change the things in my life that could be holding me back, and I wonder if you see me reacting a particular way over and over again that's counterproductive." It might take a little prodding and convincing to get them to open up, but once they understand the reason you want to know the truth, they're likely to give it to you.

Another technique is to make a list of the events in life you regret, times you wish you had acted differently or made a different decision. Go over the list again and again, looking for a theme that ties the regrets together. Actually put words to the theme. *"A lot of things on this list got here because I become afraid when projects seem as though they're growing too fast."* Or, *"A lot of things on this list got here because I become envious of people in my life and then do something to undermine my relationships."* Or, *"A lot of things on this list got here because I don't really give people clear messages when I'm not interested in them, and then I end up feeling resentful when I spend much more time with them socially or even romantically than I should."*

Think of yourself as a mystery, and then play detective. You're searching for clues—weak links in the chain of your best intentions and core truth. You are beginning to do exactly what Glenn did when he decided to reformat the hard disk of his soul to remove any software that was corrupted by viruses. You are doing the work that insight-oriented therapists like me strive to do with their patients.

Don't despair if it takes you longer than you think to put your finger on the emotional and behavioral patterns obscuring your true path. Remember, it has taken a long time for these patterns to develop, and they are camouflaged by denial. Very often, the insight you need to really begin remaking yourself will come unexpectedly. It might be while you're driving and someone says something as seemingly innocuous as "How about if we stop for lunch at that new place up ahead, instead of grabbing lunch at the mall?" You may notice that you have an initial knee-jerk reaction against the idea, maybe because you don't like new places, or maybe because you don't like changing plans, or maybe because you don't like going along with an idea that wasn't yours from the start. Whatever the pattern, it might extend far beyond a change in restaurants, to *any plan you can't control*. And that would be very, very important to note.

Major insights begin as quiet knocks on the door of denial. Just *listen* for them.

One of the most powerful techniques that I and other psychiatrists use to help patients is the ability to *listen to ourselves listening*. Psychiatrists are trained to develop a kind of "third ear" that allows us to monitor how we feel while we interact with patients. If a patient says something that makes a psychiatrist feel suddenly irritable or suddenly sad, that may be a clue that what they've just heard is connected to a meaningful theme in their life. Psychiatrists learn not to *ignore* these gut feelings, but to pay special attention to them. You can develop your own third ear to listen to yourself as you interact with others.

Try to be aware of what gut feelings visit you as you go through your day. What is your truth whispering? Don't ignore promptings from your soul that are actually knocks on the door of denial, asking you to open it, even a little, just to hear a little bit better what that whisper was all about.

STEP THREE:

Accept That Today's Negative Emotional and Behavioral Patterns Are Almost Certainly Connected to Painful Memories and Unresolved Conflicts from the Past

Other authors will tell you to focus on the moment and the power of now. We believe that you first need to understand critical moments in earlier chapters of your life story. We believe in *the power of then*.

Do you find yourself lingering to talk to the teachers when you drop your child off at school in the morning? Is that because you experienced important life events connected with your own school years? Was that the only place you felt truly safe as a child? Or could it be because think you might want to *be* a teacher, deep inside?

Do you get a gut feeling you want to move on quickly whenever anyone brings up suffering a financial setback? Do you reply with one-liners like "I'm sure it'll all work out"? If so, ask yourself why. What about that topic makes you uncomfortable? Did you survive a financial catastrophe in your home when you were a child? Does the very thought of it make you feel unsafe to this day? Have you avoided investments that could have enriched you, just because you irrationally feared they would leave you bankrupt? Have you urged your children to take safe and predictable paths through life because you suffered chaos on yours?

Do you end up in arguments with your husband over whether he might be cheating, when there is no objective evidence to support your suspicions? If so, ask yourself whether you remember cheating of one kind or another in your family as a child. Is that where the roots of your current marital conflict actually lie?

Are you a frustrated musician working as a stockbroker? Do you suffer because you can't take a leap of faith to invest more time in your passion? *Why?* Which people or what events in your life gave you the message that expressing yourself was dangerous or frivolous? Did someone in your family once fail taking a big risk?

Asking yourself why you feel the way you do in certain situations can start moving the divining rod in your soul in the direction of that crystal-clear, moving, purifying current of truth that is your birthright.

STEP FOUR:

Pray to Whatever Higher Power You Believe In

Praying that God or Nature or the Cosmos or your own internal, immeasurable reservoir of spirit allows you the courage and faith to find and then face the truth about your life broadcasts your intention to your own mind, heart, and soul and—in ways that are miraculous and beyond complete human comprehension—to the minds, hearts, and souls of others.

Glenn and I both believe that prayer actually accomplishes this. Neither one of us knows how. But that doesn't bother either one of us. We don't know any scientific explanation for why a human being would cry for another person's plight simply by reading about it or watching a television program about it. We don't know any scientific reason a soldier would face enemy fire to save the lives of American citizens he has never met. We don't know any scientific reason why people would donate their organs to strangers. We don't know any scientific reason why American doctors travel thousands of miles to treat disfigured children in countries halfway around the world. We don't know any scientific reason why one man living his life on this planet, whether he be Jesus or Gandhi or the Buddha or Martin Luther King, Jr., would so galvanize what is good and decent in people that millions would hear of his thoughts and acts and use that energy to discover something good and decent inside them.

We don't *know*. And that's okay. Because we *believe*. We have *faith*.

But we do know this: if you get on your knees and ask God for help facing the truth, you will invite and receive strength to do so.

Isn't it interesting that folks who deny the existence

of God and who would never pray for His help will often do so when their children fall ill? The reality of a son or daughter who is suffering or facing death can bring people to their knees who have never gotten on their knees before and would have sworn they never would.

You are that child. You are worthy of the same devotion and belief and hope and prayer as your own son or daughter would be when facing their own mortality. You deserve to be saved from a life of denial, separated from your truth.

So, pray for it. Let the rest of us, mystically and immeasurably, be joined to your quest.

Following this four-step plan won't solve all your problems, but it can begin to reconnect you with the sacred source of the solution to the internal obstacles in your heart and mind that keep you from knowing your*self*, speaking your mind, and pursuing your dreams.

There is no substitute for the truth. You cannot exercise free will if you do not free yourself from the past by looking honestly at your life story—painful pages included—and learning precisely who you really are.

GLENN

Isn't There Anyone to Hate?

Once I realized Tania's importance to my general sanity, I had the good sense to ask her to marry me. She had the good sense to turn me down flat. She told me that without a shared faith—a religion we both *really* believed in—we would never make it as a couple. She had seen some of my demons and she knew I needed strength from God to defeat them, once and for all. She was convinced we were going to need a spiritual anchor in our lives.

She was right, of course, but back then I didn't see it

that way. I was still searching for someone *to blame* for my suffering. I really wanted someone to transfer my hate to, so that I could stop hating myself.

I had cleansed myself of poisons like alcohol and cocaine that I had used to try to kill my real emotions—to kill my true self. Instead, I had dug deep for the roots of those emotions. And I had found plenty. That helped me feel stronger and more authentic. But it hadn't filled an especially deep, dark space inside me, a kind of cauldron where self-doubt and anger were still churning.

I was sober and I had an incredible woman in my life, but I was still the guy who had screwed up lots of professional opportunities. I was still the guy living with the aftermath of a shattered marriage. I was still a father struggling to get the parenting part of my life right. I was still the guy who had made lots of enemies. I was still underwater financially and uncertain I would ever put to good use whatever talents my mother had seen in me. I was still the guy who could sometimes *feel* like firing someone for handing me the wrong pen or saying the wrong thing at the wrong moment, even if I wouldn't actually *do* it anymore.

There was a time back when I was drinking when I had wished that Pat—my best friend in the world, the man who kept reminding me that I was a better person than I believed—would hit a rough patch in his life. And even though I wasn't drinking, that thought hadn't completely left me. Part of me still wanted him to veer off track. He was always so positive. He weathered storms with such grace. It made me painfully aware of my own shortcomings. And since this book is all about the truth, it made me . . . *angry.*

When you aren't drinking or using drugs or spending lots of money on fancy toys or basking in the glow of fame or working all the time or eating your way through the refrigerator, being hateful and angry is a very handy shield from the truth. It lets you focus on everyone else's shortcomings, and all the ways they've let you down. You can bemoan how all these broken people keep *finding* you somehow. That way you don't have to focus on what really matters—the tough work of fixing what is broken inside *you.*

I now realize that each of us attracts the kind of energy we give off. It sounds simple, but it really is true. When I was at my worst, I attracted bad influences and made bad decisions. When I was at my best, the opposite was true.

I'd say I was lucky to be so close to Pat, but by now you probably know that *lucky* isn't a word I put too much value in anymore. Our relationship was far more bread crumb than happenstance. Pat was unshakably convinced he was on to something about me that was redeeming.

There was another supposed friend of mine back

then—a person to whom I owed some money. At one point, after realizing that my parents were in more financial trouble than I thought, I approached this person and said, "Listen, I'm having a really tough time keeping a roof over my head because I found out that my parents are visiting a soup kitchen and I really need to help them out for a little while. So I was wondering if maybe we could reduce my payment, maybe by five hundred a month—just for now until I can make sure they are okay."

His response? "No, sorry."

"I'm not sure you understand. My parents are eating in a soup kitchen and I just don't know if I can . . ."

"No—and I will take you to court if you try anything."

"Huh? You'd try to have me put in *jail*?"

"That's not up to me, Glenn. It's up to the judge."

I couldn't quite believe what I was hearing and I really needed some leeway, so I swallowed my pride and said, "I get it. Look, I owe you the money, there's no question about it. I've never denied that and I'm not denying it now. I will pay everything I owe, but if you could just let me pay a little less now until everyone is back on their feet, I'll make it up later. What about cutting three hundred a month for now, that would really . . ."

"No."

"Not three hundred?" I knew it wasn't my place to judge anyone else's situation. Maybe I didn't know something about some kind of financial jam this fellow was in. I was near tears, but I held them back. "A hundred, then? Could we—just for now, not forever, okay, but, maybe, like, for six months—go down a hundred a month?"

Again, he just shook his head. "I want all my money the day it's due, every month. That's what I'm entitled to and that's the way it's going to be."

He was right. He *was* entitled to it. I was finally getting the message. It wasn't that he didn't believe I was in a really bad spot. It wasn't about him needing the money I was paying. It was the fact that he had the power to insist on every bit of it, exactly on schedule, and didn't care what my circumstances were. He had absolutely zero compassion for me.

Something about that feeling and that moment made me want to define it in an absolute way, maybe because I still couldn't accept it. "How about a dollar less a month?" I said. "One dollar."

"Not a dollar, Glenn. Not a penny." His face turned red. "I want it all. Every single cent! You're going to give it to me right on time, or we're going to go to court and let the law take it from there. You got it?"

I nodded. "Yes, I get it," I said. "I understand. You won't help me."

"Get me what you owe me, when you're supposed to, and we'll have no problems."

I was floored. Just to be perfectly clear, I'd agreed to pay this money and it was my duty to honor it. Legally, he did not need to move one inch for me; I was just surprised and hurt that he didn't *want* to.

But while that incident changed our relationship, it didn't change our agreement. So I paid him every month. I paid him when I couldn't buy gas or do my laundry or buy food. I paid him every penny, just like he'd demanded. Each time I did, a part of me felt like I must be a really bad soul, deep down, to be reaping the kind of heartlessness he kept showing me.

Then the unexpected happened: I was told something about this person that could be very damaging. I mean, it was the kind of information that, if his business partners knew, would really embarrass him—badly. What he'd done wasn't technically illegal, but it was so shady that he would have been drummed out of business, just on appearances. I thought to myself, *What goes around comes around, doesn't it? Now, we'll see who ends up groveling.* I thought about how weak and ashamed I had felt begging him to let me pay a hundred bucks less each month. And it's amazing how quickly that weakness and shame flipped into anger and a desire for retribution.

He lived a few hours away, and I wanted to tell him

face-to-face exactly what I'd learned and what I planned to do with the information.

I got into my car with Tania and started driving. She could see I was feeling a lot better than I had in a while. After all, I was a man on a mission. I was going to *enjoy* this. I went over the whole story with her on the way. How I had tested him by asking him for a reduction of one dollar a month in what I owed him. *One dollar.* And how he'd refused. He had kicked me hard when I was down.

She just listened.

I told her what I knew about him and how I didn't want to just call his partners with the information, because I wanted to actually see his face when he heard what I was about to tell them.

"Why?" she asked.

"Why what?"

"Why do you want to see it in person?"

"You're kidding, right? Didn't I just tell you how badly he *hurt* me?"

"And hurting him back is going to do exactly what? I'm not trying to rain on your parade or anything. I mean, I know you've been up at night worrying about money. I know you have trouble focusing at work. I guess you want him to suffer like you have—that's kind of the long and short of it, right?"

Something about the way she asked that, so simply, in a voice filled with kindness, took the wind out of my sails. "Well, he didn't care that I . . ."

"Nope. You're absolutely right . . . didn't care one bit." She looked straight ahead.

Okay, then, I thought to myself. *We're on the same page.* I hit the gas a little harder.

"I wonder what happened to make him so cruel," she said.

I glanced at her.

"I'm not saying you should do anything or not do anything," she said. "You have every right to be really angry. I was just wondering. What do you figure turned him into someone who would demand every single cent he's owed from someone who's barely getting by?"

"Do I really have to do this?" I asked.

"No," she said softly. "It's *really* your choice."

I wish you knew Tania, because only then could you understand how she can say a simple sentence like that. There's nothing demanding in it, barely even a hint of ex-pectation. It's more like hope. She hopes you will turn out to be the person she believes you can be. And it can cut to the very heart of you very quickly and cleanly.

"Someone who was once . . . cheated," I said.

"Cheated out of money . . . ," she led.

"I mean, that's what this is all about. Right?"

"Well, it sure *seems* that way."

I didn't even have to look at her to know that she was waiting patiently for me to stop being so concrete in my thinking. "It wouldn't have to be money," I said. "He could have been cheated out of anything valuable."

"Even love, I guess. I'm not trying to be all sappy, but I can see how a person could feel like they've got no love and that getting every single dollar they can will make up for it."

Something about that sounded sort of familiar. "Maybe," I said.

She shrugged. "Interesting . . ."

Point taken. I pulled the car into the right-hand lane and slowed down a bit. "I should have taken this drive alone. You don't make revenge any fun."

"How much fun is it, really, to break an already broken person? How does that help you become the person *you* want to be?"

I took the next exit, turned around, and headed back toward home. I didn't say anything for a full minute or so.

"You okay?" Tania asked, finally.

"Oh, yeah." I was better than okay. I was more sure than ever that I was with my soul mate. "I think we need to find that religion we both believe in, sooner rather than later," I said.

Tania just smiled.

The two of us, together with my daughters, ended up embarking on what we now refer to as "the Beck Family Church Tour." We visited a Unitarian church. We went to a Presbyterian church. We went to a Unity church. We went to a synagogue. We went to an Episcopalian church. We even went to a church that didn't mention God at all. I kid you not. Halfway through the service the pastor announced, "You all know that I don't believe there's a God, but if there were one, we should serve him."

Tania and I just looked at one another. Uh, no, we hadn't known that about the pastor.

Then, one day, Pat called me out of the blue. "Are you really doing a church tour?" he asked.

"Yes," I told him.

"Glenn," he said, "how long have we been friends?"

Pat has that same sort of loving, direct way that Tania does of telegraphing how you could be a better person, or a better friend. So I knew what was coming. "Obviously, too long," I joked.

"How long have we been friends, Glenn?"

"A long time, Pat," I said.

"You owe it to me. You owe it to yourself to make a stop at the Church of Jesus Christ of Latter-day Saints."

I really didn't want to go. I mean, those people were freaks. Sure, none of the Mormons I *knew* personally was a freak, but I had a preconceived notion to protect. I had

tried to keep my distance from Mormons ever since finding myself essentially surrounded by them on my first job
in radio—right after high school—in Seattle. "Sorry, Pat,
you just missed us. We've been going in alphabetical order
and you should have come in right after B'nai-i-Jacob."

"I'm serious."

"Okay . . . Okay. In all seriousness, then, I'm not
going."

"Remember *The Silence of the Lambs?*" he said. "You
owe me one."

He was really pulling out all the stops, reminding me
of *that*. See, the Church of Latter-day Saints encourages
members to see films about uplifting, inspiring characters.
Hannibal Lecter really doesn't qualify. But somehow, during a very dark hour in my life, when I was drunk a good
deal of the time, I convinced him to go with me to see
The Silence of the Lambs. Looking back, I probably resonated with a character like the one Jodi Foster played, a
character who needs to revisit the traumas of her past and
become the person she has the potential to be, in order to
do battle with evil. I had already seen the film the week
before and told him it really wasn't that gory or violent.

I remember looking at him halfway through the
movie. All the blood had drained from his face.

"You don't think *this* is bad?" he whispered.

"Well, I didn't notice it the first time around, but I

guess I am now seeing it through your eyes, and, yeah, it is kind of dark, huh?"

That was the last R-rated film Pat ever went to see.

I figured he had a point: If he had sat through a serial killer film to hang out with me when I was down, I should be able to sit through a church service for him.

"Okay, Pat," I said, "because of you, I'll go." I still needed my peculiar sense of humor as a shield. "But I want to emphasize that the dogs of Hell could not drag me into Mormonism. You people are nuts and have way too many rules. But I'll go as a favor to you. So what time does it start?"

"Well, that's a great attitude to go in with. It's Sunday from ten till one."

What? Three hours? At church? I needed a faith, not a part-time job. Three hours seemed like way too much time for any sensible religious service. If you can't help me show my devotion to God in sixty minutes or less, then count me out. But I did owe Pat that favor. I told my kids and Tania that we'd make an appearance and be out in an hour.

It didn't happen that way. I tried to leave after an hour, but Tania ended up chatting with some of the folks attending the service, and one thing led to another, and we ended up in a class called Gospel Principles.

I don't remember what the teacher was talking about,

but all of a sudden, someone raised a hand and said, "Hey, I don't understand that."

I looked at Tania, then at the teacher, then back at Tania. "Wait a minute," I said, grinning like a Cheshire cat. "You can ask questions here."

"Don't you dare embarrass me," she said.

I raised my hand, and I had a good question. (By "good" I mean a question that I thought would have me in the car and on the way to the McDonald's drive-through within five minutes.) It was designed to convince myself that I was with people who espoused only limited forgiveness. Once I had that evidence in hand, I could walk. That seems pretty transparent to me now, given how desperately I needed genuine and complete forgiveness in my life.

"Yes, Mr. Beck?" the teacher said.

"Where's Gandhi?" I asked.

"Pardon me?"

"Where is Gandhi? He didn't accept Jesus as his savior, so is he burning in Hell?" I waited for the answer I expected—that Gandhi was an exemplary person, but that, yes, he had, sadly, been condemned to eternal damnation.

"Well, who would like to answer that?" the teacher asked the class.

A fellow student said, "If a loving father asked his

son to lead a good and decent life, and when he turned eighteen and graduated from high school, told him to make sure he went to college, but there were no colleges where he lived, or no college would accept him because he wasn't the right 'sort' . . . would that loving father then condemn the son, or disown him, for not having gone to college?"

"Well, wait a minute," I said. "Didn't Jesus say there is no way to the Father but through him?"

"Yes, that is true," replied the student, "but would it be fair for one who had never had the chance or opportunity to accept Him to be banished to that lake of fire?"

That resonated with me because of the many years I had been stalked by God. I mean, even just in the years I'd known Pat, I'd been given one opportunity after another to take him up on the chorus he kept singing in the background of my self-loathing: *Glenn, you're a better person than you imagine. I have some answers, if you'll listen.* I had just never been in a state of mind or spirit where I really had the free will to knowingly accept or reject his offer.

If Pat had not been the one to finally turn the key, would my Father in Heaven have continued to stalk me or would my chances have all been exhausted? Latter-day Saints do not believe that your chances ever cease, even with death. They end only with full understanding and denial of truth by your own exercise of real free will. And even then there is no "lake of fire." There is just the Hell that is realizing you *could* have been with your loved ones and your Heavenly Father and His Son, but you're not. That is far worse than any "lake of fire."

As we were leaving the church, I began thinking that I might have to explore this Mormonism thing further. After a McDonald's run, of course, and a cup of coffee. That's when my two daughters said, "Can we go back there?"

"What?" I asked.

"Can we go back there? To that church."

"Um, okay," I said.

My eldest daughter, Mary, who has always had a spiritual gift, said, "I just feel so warm inside."

My younger daughter Hannah then said, "Yeah, you know, I felt different in there."

That was the first time that had ever happened. I don't mean just to me, I mean in the entire history of civilization. Kids *asking* to go to church? So we went back.

The next time there, I took Thomas Jefferson's advice: I questioned *everything* I could think to question about the faith. I went over my doubts again and again with the church bishop. I read everything there was to read on their website and every word of *Mormon Doctrine*. I treated Mormonism as if it were a hostile witness. For a

while I went to the anti-Mormon literature for hints, but I
I found most of it to be unfair or just plain wrong. I tried
every trick I could think of to find a contradiction.

The problem was that I couldn't. Mormonism seemed
to explain the world and my place in it better than any
other faith I had looked at. It answered many spiritual
questions that had gone unanswered for me for my entire life. It seemed to work *for me* as a unique individual,
looking to keep the hard drive of my soul clean. Free of
anything that didn't truly have pristine code and might
corrupt the rest of the software. *For me.*

You'll notice that I've written the words *for me* a few
times. That's not because my thesaurus isn't close by; it's
because each of us has to find the particular lens that fo-
cuses his or her spiritual vision, and *for me* that seemed to
be Mormonism.

The fact is that you can't become the powerful person
God hopes you will if you try to pretend you believe in
things you don't really believe in. Or if you try to pretend
you like your work when you don't. Or you try to pretend
you're in a relationship in which you're loved when you're
just not.

Remember, when God sent Moses to the Pharaoh he
named himself I AM, which has also been translated as *He
Who Is Ever Becoming What He Is.*

That means *you*, too. Your path is to forever evolve

into your*self*, to always be striving to become the person you are supposed to be.

I think the true point at which the last of my lingering doubts left came when my family and I were sitting with a man at the church whom I had unkindly nicknamed the Amazing Mr. Plastic Man. I called him that (never to his face) because he was so happy and so welcoming of us and I just didn't see how it could be possible that he was genuinely that way. I assumed he was either high on something, in deep denial, or just completely insane. Anyway, we were sitting in a Sunday-school class, discussing Zion, the Mormon concept of a place and condition where "all are pure in heart." It's a place where people earn as much money as their talents allow, but take only the amount they need and give the rest to help the poor, widowed, or fatherless. In Zion, people really care about one another. It's not socialism; it's the exact opposite. No heart is forced to do anything. Every single heart chooses to help others because of their own free will.

We spent an hour talking about Zion, and after the Amazing Mr. Plastic Man got to the end he said, "Now, brother, how do we do it?"

How do we do it? I thought to myself. *How does it happen? How was it remotely possible that this actually could happen?*

People raised their hands and gave their answers. Then

the Amazing Mr. Plastic Man welled up and said, "There's only one way this will happen: if I truly love you and you truly love me. If deep down inside of ourselves we see people for who they really are: our literal brothers and sisters. We may not like them, we may not like what they're doing, but we love them."

He was crying and I was crying, because that was the simple truth I'd been looking for—not God in theory, but God in practice—and it reached to the core of both of us.

Compassion isn't easy. It's a lot harder to love people than to judge them. Sometimes it's a lot harder to love them than it is to hate them. We get confused by what we see them doing in the world—some of it unattractive, some of it downright ugly—instead of focusing on what they *could* do, if they could follow the bread crumbs and find their paths to embracing the truth.

While I had forgiven my mother on that Christmas Eve, I don't think I came face-to-face with the full weight of losing her until I found my faith. Until then, my anger was still partly in the way. I couldn't fully empathize with the sadness she must have experienced in order to lose the will to live, even when her son adored her, even when her daughters still thirsted for more of her love, and her husband still needed her.

As my anger dissolved, my grief increased. But I didn't

fight it. I didn't deny it. I let myself feel it. And it did not destroy me. It made me stronger.

That's the power of compassion.

I reached out to my father. I wanted to understand how the early chapters in his life story had impacted him once he was a married man with children and, later, after his ex-wife killed herself. The painful recollections he shared with me made me understand a lot better something he had told me back when I was ten.

"At some point," he told me, "a father puts the ball down on the field and then it's the son's job to pick it up and carry it the rest of the way."

Well, let me tell you this: With what I learned about my father's childhood, he carried the ball a miraculously long way, given the performance of *his* father. He had to have been a very, very strong person to have stayed on his feet for so many yards.

I would never have known any of that, had I kept my distance from my father out of anger. I never would have known *him*. When I vowed to start trying to have a real relationship with my father, we made a promise to one another: We would sit through the awkward silences. When we felt uncomfortable, we wouldn't change the subject. Saying that out loud to each other made all the difference in the world. Awkward silence is a lot less awkward when you've both acknowledged its existence.

Defeat anger, stop using it as a shield against truth, and you will find the compassion you need to forgive the people you love. Believe me, those people will be much tougher to forgive than strangers, because they are the ones who had the capacity to hurt you the most.

See, when you strip everything else away, there really is no one to hate. As Keith likes to say, "There's no original sin left in the world. Everyone's just recycling pain now."

You can't love your mother or father if you don't also have the capacity to grieve their deaths and, perhaps even more so, grieve parts of their lives. You can't hope for happiness without honest confrontation with what might cause you suffering and tears. Try to have one without the other, and you'll have nothing.

No one to hate. It ended up that there was really only one person left in the whole world I still needed to make certain those four words applied to. And that person was yours truly. I had been working hard to forgive myself for a lot of my shortcomings. I had made some peace with the fact that I had lived a life of ego and fear and that I had done harm to myself and to others. I had searched my life history for the roots of a lot of my shortcomings so that I could make real changes in the hope of no longer repeating the same damaging patterns. But I couldn't shake that last, stubborn worry that I was not fully worthy of good things happening to me because I had been doing bad things for such a long time.

I still felt something cold and empty at my very core.

That's where the atonement came in—at least it did *for me*.

I believe the atonement is the most powerful thing in the world. Christ's sacrifice of his life to atone for mankind's sins literally means that each and every one of us can actually close that final distance between forgiving ourselves and *being* forgiven completely, for all eternity, so that anything becomes possible again.

The story that includes Christ's suffering on the cross begins with him essentially saying, "Look, I'll satisfy the justice thing. I'll go down there and take on all the sins and all the stains so everyone who is truly ready can have a clean slate, a real second chance." My faith teaches that it isn't just our *sins* Christ suffered and died for, but also our sorrows, our disappointments, heartaches, and embarrassments. All of it. That's why he says, even as he is being crucified, "Father, forgive them, they know not what they are doing."

When we really screw up, we *can't* forgive ourselves—not all the way. We're all a little like kids who do things that are wrong. *Very* wrong. *Lots* of things. We lie. We withhold love. We manipulate. We are unkind to others and ourselves. And we want to avoid looking at our Father at all costs. We think He won't love us anymore. But that's true Hell. And it's a tragedy. Because He's not just waiting to dispense justice, He's waiting to forgive you. He's the polar opposite of that older "friend" of mine who refused to lower my debt by even a dollar a month. He'll wipe your debt clean the second you ask. Gone. You just have to know in your heart of hearts that it's possible that you are a literal son or daughter of God who is inherently worthwhile.

God is your spiritual dad. He's the source of the immeasurable, indomitable power that waits inside you—no matter how long you have wandered in search of it, no matter how lost you think you are. That's the truth.

That's why we must never forsake one another. We must have compassion for others and for ourselves. Because I am quite literally your brother, and you are quite literally my brothers and sisters.

That is the great thing about God. He *is* chained to the truth. If He says do *this* and I promise *that* will happen, it must be true or He ceases to be God.

My life changed after I understood and accepted the atonement. My focus changed. I changed. The guy firing people because of the Sharpie wasn't just silenced now; he was dead and buried. Where once I was focused only on Money, Booze, Business, and Cars, I now wanted to focus only on People and Family.

That doesn't mean I don't still fail. I do, and many times I'm lucky enough to do it in front of millions of people. But today I understand that while I can't be perfect, I believe faith and family have allowed me to make failure the exception rather than the rule. The change I needed was there the whole time I was looking for it. I just needed to look in the right place. Finding what worked *for me* made all the difference. Finding what works *for you* will do the same.

KEITH

The Fourth Wonder: Compassion

Somewhere along the line, having compassion for others who make big mistakes in life—especially mistakes that hurt us or those we care about—got mixed up with accommodating their shortcomings or simply excusing their behavior. In the minds of some people, the act of *understanding* became synonymous with being weak and gave compassion a bad name.

That's a shame, because compassion is one of the most empowering human emotions. It allows us to demonstrate strength by keeping our sights focused on the higher standards to which we can all aspire and by ensuring we feel sorrow when anyone among us falls short.

Glenn's compassion for his father and mother, despite their weaknesses, didn't weaken him or make him more vulnerable to being hurt in the future. Neither did his compassion for the person who had demanded that he pay his debt in full, every month, even if it meant that he would go hungry. It demonstrated his faith that human beings have the inborn capacity to do better and that when they don't realize that potential, their failings are worthy of mourning for what could have been. Glenn's compassion kept him from getting lost in anger or blame or hatred, veering away from his own path toward truth. It let him keep seeking and celebrating the source of light in the world, rather than depleting himself by despising the shadows.

Anger, blame, and hatred take tremendous energy to sustain. It's like trying to get somewhere while walking into hurricane-force winds. Compassion, on the other hand, is wind at your back and sun falling warmly on your face. It makes not only for an easier journey, but for a much more pleasant one as well.

Vaclav Havel, poet, playwright, dissident, and first president of the Czech Republic, put it this way:

⚬◈◈⚬

Hate has a lot in common with love, chiefly with that self-transcending aspect of love, the fixation on others, the dependence on them and in fact the delegation of a piece of one's own identity to them. . . . The hater longs for the object of his hatred.

⚬◈◈⚬

Break free of that longing. Don't let yourself be derailed by hardening your heart. Use compassion to stay on the path to your own truth, because every time you go beyond labeling anyone as bad or reprehensible or evil and instead resolve to understand *why* he or she has wandered into darkness—what *happened* to shatter that person—you remind yourself that nothing in the world is beyond human comprehension. You invite immeasurable power into your life—the power of hope and wisdom and understanding; the power of God. And, in not too long, you will have all the confidence you need to turn and face any demon from the past that has had you on the run.

No one ends up destroying himself or anyone else out of the blue—out of real free *choice*, true agency. Trace the life history of any such person and you will find the reasons *why* they lost their God-given capacity to love and respect themselves and others.

This holds true in every single case. There is no one born empty of his or her God-given potential, with nothing worth redeeming at core. There is no infant delivered evil, out of the womb. There never has been. Not even one. Don't believe me? Go find a friend with a three-month-old child and look into that child's eyes. Pure innocence. Pure potential. There is no hate, no sorrow, grief, or anger (except maybe at 3 A.M. when they want to eat)—there is only love, wonder, and light. It is our experiences that shape us, bend us, and yes, sometimes even break us. But remember, you were once that three-month-old child full of God's love and grace—the only thing stopping you from being that again is you.

That's why every story of a person who has lost compassion for others or who feels little or nothing when causing others to suffer is the tragic story of a person who was himself overwhelmed by traumatic events—*dehumanized* by them, crushed by them.

Yes, *every* story, with no exception. Ever. Charles Manson was not born evil. Ted Bundy wasn't. The BTK killer wasn't. Hitler wasn't. Every single man or woman who has acted without empathy has had that God-given miracle destroyed by having enough pain visited upon them, in the setting of enough helplessness, to extinguish it. In order to become a murderer a person first has to have been spiritually murdered.

You may remember the story of Scott Peterson, the Modesto, California, man who, on Christmas Eve of 2002, reported his pregnant wife, Laci, missing, then led the search for her. In fact, Peterson had killed Laci and disposed of her body in San Francisco Bay. He'd been having an affair at that time with a massage therapist named Amber Frey.

What other explanation could there be for a man killing his pregnant wife on Christmas Eve other than being born with pure evil inside?

In my book *Inside the Mind of Scott Peterson*, I think I provide a much more credible answer. Scott Peterson was taught that human life—including his own—had no value. Back in 1945, his maternal grandfather was murdered for about five hundred dollars by a disgruntled former employee. Peterson's mother, Jackie, was only two years old at the time. Despite her own mother still being alive (though widowed), she was placed in an orphanage that has since been called a "cesspool of pedophilia."

When she left that orphanage as a teenager she gave birth to two children out of wedlock and quickly put them up for adoption. She didn't give it a lot of thought. She finally married Lee Peterson, a man who had divorced his wife partly because he didn't like the kids they'd had together. Together, Lee and Jackie had a baby. They named him Scott.

There was just one small problem: they had a funny habit of leaving him behind in places like a neighborhood restaurant, where the manager would have to call out to them, "Jackie! Lee! You left Scott!"

That's just one part of Scott Peterson's ugly biography. Sound like the kind of life story that leads a person to value a mother? A baby? Or does it sound like the kind of life story that leads to the creation of a person who instinctively despises new life?

What good does it do us to hate Scott Peterson? Or Charles Manson? What injury could it do us to understand them and the tragic destruction of human empathy they represent?

Many people have spoken about compassion over the years:

- "You will not be punished for your anger," the Buddha said. "You will be punished by your anger."
- "Tears shed for self are tears of weakness, but tears shed for others are a sign of strength," the late Baptist evangelist Billy Graham said.

- "Compassion will prove the means to liberation," Hindu scripture tells us.
- "Compassion is the anti-toxin of the soul," the late philosopher Eric Hoffer wrote. "Where there is compassion even the most poisonous impulses remain relatively harmless."
- "If a way to the better there be, it lies in taking a full look at the worst," wrote Thomas Hardy, the late novelist and poet.

People are inherently good. Our souls are magnificent and capable of extraordinary performance. But human beings are also exquisitely fragile—especially in childhood. When we are visited by cruelty or catastrophe or neglect, the spiritual structure of our humanity can sustain fractures. Sometimes these are hairline fractures that need bracing and time to heal. But sometimes they are complete breaks that lead people to limp through life, or to always veer in the wrong direction, or to lean on others inappropriately, or worse.

When you refuse to be blinded by the weaknesses, cruelties, and even, dare I say, the atrocities of others, and instead begin to focus on the source of their failings, you celebrate and may just strengthen the parts of them that are linked to God, and you certainly strengthen those parts within yourself.

I could provide many examples to illustrate true compassion, but one dramatic story that comes to mind is the compassion shown by the Amish people for Charles Carl Roberts IV and his family.

Roberts took ten Amish girls, ages six to thirteen, hostage at a one-room schoolhouse in the community of Nickel Mines in Lancaster County, Pennsylvania, on October 2, 2006. He bound and terrorized the girls before shooting five of them to death, then killing himself.

Despite their grief, the Amish community almost immediately reached out to the killer's family, expressing their forgiveness and even visiting them to offer comfort. Amish mourners at Roberts's funeral outnumbered the non-Amish in attendance. And the Roberts family was invited to attend a funeral of one of the girls who had been murdered.

Why would the Amish behave this way? Because they understand the tragedy it is—even for the person who falls from Grace—when a human being with the inherent potential to express love and to honor God instead becomes destructive.

Did this weaken the Amish community of Nickel Mines? Did it invite more killings? I don't believe either to be true. Much to the contrary, Glenn and I believe, as do the Amish people, that refusing to harbor hatred and being intent on expressing compassion empowers and protects them.

Compassion is a force for good, not a capitulation to that which is bad.

In every arena of life, knowing the underlying cause of a malfunction is critical to correcting it or at least to preventing it from doing even more damage. In order to treat physical illnesses or safeguard the community from transmissible ones, doctors need to know their *pathophysiology*— how the disease causes its chaos in the human body. It certainly wouldn't do to simply *hate* the illness or flee it. Only understanding it leads to the ability to eventually triumph over it.

The same is true for fixing a car. Kicking it won't help. Cursing at it won't help. Pretending all is well and grinding its gears until you drive it into the ground won't help. Only getting under the hood and *understanding* what has gone wrong allows for rational solutions to fix it.

The act of *understanding* defeats illnesses and mechanical problems and environmental problems and problems in the economy. The act of compassion defeats human problems of the soul as well.

Never be afraid to *feel* for someone else, no matter how *unfeeling* they have been to you. When you do, you stand with what is good and decent and miraculous. You stand with God.

Do you want to know how powerful compassion can be, even when looked at through the limiting lens of science? When people are suffering with major depression, research has shown that a type of nuclear medicine scan called positron emission tomography (PET) can often reveal specific regions of their brains with decreased metabolic activity—a reduced flow of chemical messengers between nerve cells. In other words, their brains are partly shut down in certain anatomic locations.

When antidepressant medications are effective, PET scans show that metabolic activity—energy flow—has been restored in those places. But here's the really amazing thing: when psychotherapy is effective, the previously sluggish areas in the brains of depressed individuals also show that metabolism is restored to normal.

Think about that for a bit. When these findings were reported in medical journals, they were presented merely as evidence that psychotherapy can be as effective as medications in impacting the pathophysiology of major depression at the level of the brain. But nowhere in the journals was there a scientist who seemed taken aback by the sheer wonder of what these results revealed!

Why? This is an astounding discovery! These studies prove that someone listening in a compassionate way to another human being's life story can actually *alter that person's brain chemistry* in a healing way. Compassion can change the brain's metabolism so that energy flow has been restored.

Do you think compassion changes only the brains

of those who are depressed and not the brains of those who connect with them and heal them? I would wager everything I own that that is not the case. When we are compassionate toward others not only are our souls strengthened, but our bodies are as well. Literally, every molecule in our bodies registers our alignment with God.

Can anyone really doubt anymore that we have the ability to change lives—including our own—when we empower ourselves with compassion?

When I was hosting a daily syndicated talk show, a big, hulking man named Larry and his three adult daughters once came on as guests. Larry's daughters had reached out to the show producers because they wanted to confront their father publicly about the way he had treated them as children. They remembered him punishing them brutally, but he had always refused to admit that, arguing that they had talked each other into exaggerating an occasional spanking into something far more sinister. The women had decided that it hurt them too much to listen to him continue to deny their reality. They even insisted on sitting a short distance away from him on the set so that they wouldn't feel threatened by him. But they wanted to give their father one more chance to admit what had happened before saying goodbye to him—forever.

For most of the time that Larry was on the program he dodged and weaved around the rather hazy memories his daughters presented. Yes, he admitted, the spankings might have been a little too hard for girls, but he had disciplined them out of love. Okay, so maybe there had been a time or two he was drunk, but that never affected his judgment and wouldn't be affecting his memory.

Then one of Larry's daughters made everything quite clear. Trembling, with tears in her eyes but strength in her voice, she said, "I wasn't going to bring this up, okay? But I'm not going to keep it in anymore. I just can't. Because it won't do me any good and it won't do my sisters any good and it won't do you any good, either. So, listen to me: Are you saying that you didn't go into the backyard and get a tree branch and beat us with it when we were children? Is that what you're saying? Because if it is, then this is the last time you'll see us or speak to us."

"You did, Dad," one of the other women said quietly. "More than once. And we hadn't even done anything wrong."

Then all three women's eyes filled up with tears.

Folks in the studio audience whispered audibly to one another and shook their heads cynically.

Larry fell silent. He shrugged, gazed out at the audience, and then looked defiantly at me.

I met this lumbering, aging fellow's eyes. "Life isn't fair," I told him. "We don't have days or weeks to work this out. We have this hour, no more, and most of it's already gone."

Larry stared back at me, silent.

"So how about it?" I went on. "Your daughters say you went into the backyard and got a tree branch and beat them with it. That wouldn't make you the Devil, but it would mean you lost control and you were cruel—not once, either. More than once. They say they won't see you again or talk to you again if you don't agree. But if it didn't happen, or you don't remember it happening, you *shouldn't* agree. You should just tell the truth. That's all you can do."

Several seconds passed. Then Larry's chin began to quiver, and tears filled his eyes. "It's not as bad as what happened to me as a kid," he said to me.

The three women were speechless, leaning forward in their chairs, listening. The whispers in the studio audience ceased. The room was completely, utterly silent.

How did that revelation by a long-ago guest of mine affect you reading it just now? Did you just sigh knowingly or feel your skin turn to gooseflesh or remember something about your own life experience that resonates with what those girls and their father expressed? Because if you were affected in any of those ways or in any similar way, then you were just touched by one of the most amazing forces in the universe: compassion for other human beings.

"Tell *them*," I said to Larry, nodding at Larry's daughters.

Larry hesitated, but then his shoulders fell, tears started down his cheeks, and he turned to them. "It's not as bad as what happened to me as a kid," he repeated.

It's not as bad as what happened to me as a kid. Twelve words, spoken after decades, and suddenly everything changed for a father and his three daughters who had been distant for years and on the verge of complete estrangement. Because for the first time, that father was not only admitting the truth about his daughters' lives, but also sharing the truth about his own. In an instant, the distance between them collapsed. I could feel it happen.

Compassion will do that. Compassion is a miracle.

The daughter who had issued the ultimatum to her father spoke for all three women. "We never knew you had been . . . We had no idea."

"I know," Larry said. "I know. And I'm sorry I didn't deal with it. I'm sorry for what I did to you. I'm so sorry." He stood up and walked toward his daughters.

And then another miracle happened. His daughters stood up, surrounded him, and held him while he cried.

As I quoted earlier, the Reverend Billy Graham once said, "Tears shed for self are tears of weakness, but tears shed for others are a sign of strength."

You might think that Larry was healed that day. You might think that his three daughters were healed that day. But if that is all you think happened, you're missing the magic of how compassion works, because I was also touched and changed by it. No doubt many people in the audience were, too. And we'll never know how many of the people watching at home were as well.

Compassion is contagious because it is linked to the truth. And the truth is all-powerful. It transcends time and space and heals people in mystical, immeasurable ways that we still understand precious little about.

Having heard about Larry and his daughters, you yourself might feel like being even more honest with someone close to you, or more curious about that person's life story, or more forgiving. Do you see how inexplicably wonderful that would be? How instantaneously that could change the direction of multiple lives for the better?

Think of all the things that had to happen for Larry's story to reach you via this book: I had to have a talk show (one chance in several million). Larry and his daughters had to appear on it (again, the odds were small). Glenn needed to be hired for a national television show (one in tens of millions) and have me on as a guest. Then he and I needed to become colleagues, then friends, then coauthors. You needed to purchase or borrow or stumble upon a copy of what we created and you needed to reach this page and read these very words at this very moment—when you can really use them. The odds of all that happening have more zeroes than our national debt. Do you really think it was all a series of meaningless coincidences? We don't.

We suspect you are about to use compassion in your own life, to complement the wonders of courage, faith, and truth, along with others we're going to tell you about.

None of our views on compassion should be taken to mean that we advocate forgiving people for harming others without them facing the consequences of their actions. Compassion does not mean that justice need not be served. We can be compassionate about the traumas suffered in childhood even by someone who, in part because of those traumas, grows up to become a murderer. But that does not mean the murderer goes free. Much to the contrary, once we look honestly at the horribly fractured psyche in that individual or someone who rapes or someone who abuses children or someone who blows up a building full of innocent people or someone who defrauds others of their life savings, we realize the very real danger such people represent in society and the very real need to contain them—sometimes forever. But when we do so, we must not hobble ourselves by hating them.

You can pity someone and still punish that person. You can forgive someone and still resolve to keep yourself safe from any further injury from that person's pathology.

In Larry's case, we would never have advised that his daughters have him babysit their children, even after his very moving revelation. It's tragic when people are broken in childhood, or at any other time, but the fact that they have suffered and that we can resonate with their suffering does not mean they aren't potentially dangerous. Protecting ourselves and those we love is imperative.

Someone who contracts virulent, medication-resistant tuberculosis isn't *to blame* for having it. But at the point at which that individual can't show enough good judgment or concern for others to not infect them, he or she needs to be placed in quarantine and to stay there until there is reliable evidence that no one will be harmed. Period.

So it is for those infected by cruelty or violence or sociopathy. We seek to understand these things *first* in order to contain them and *only then* in order to heal them.

It is no different with virulent, damaging, false ideas and arguments that could infect you, your family, or our society. We believe it is imperative to protect yourself through knowledge and steeling yourself with the courage to fight for what you believe in. But we also think it is imperative that you not fall into the trap of hating the ideas or the folks who espouse them. Cultivate the compassion to look at the roots of even the most wrong-minded opinions. Figure out from where they came, why they appeal to certain groups or individuals, and how you might even be able to reach the people voicing them to kindle greater insight.

The late Ernest Holmes, an internationally recognized authority on religious psychology, described the power of deploying understanding on the world stage—listening for truth and standing firmly for it, rather than reacting with rage to untruths:

Gandhi built his whole philosophy of life around the theory of nonviolence [compassion's close cousin]. An ancient Chinese sage said that all things are possible to the person who can perfectly practice inaction. And the Bible exclaims: "Be still, and know that I am God." Surely some great truth must be contained in these simple thoughts. There is a spiritual consciousness that, through the power of nonresistance, can change a condition that appears solid. By way of illustration let us think of an iceberg. When the sun's rays daily fall on it, it will dissolve; that which was an obstruction becomes liquid. Such is the power of nonviolence.

There is something flowing in, around and through all things that nothing can resist. This is the something that the great and the wise have known about and have used, but too often our way is the

way of resistance [close cousin of rage and hatred].
We try to change the outer without changing the
inner first.

◦◦◦

Practicing compassion for others—whether relatives or strangers, whether in the face of destructive acts or destructive ideas—will not only help you change the people who are the objects of your compassion, not only prevent you from diminishing yourself through rage and hatred, but will also set the stage for you to be compassionate with yourself.

This is the greatest gift. This is the gift of the atonement, the power of redemption. When you accept the immeasurable power of God into your life, you are forgiven—all the way to the very real, still present, incorruptible core of your being. If you are a poet who takes up a pen after thirty years spent trying to become wealthy, you are forgiven, and your art is still yours to express. If you are a father or mother who opens your arms, heart, and mind to your children after thirty years spent making mistake after mistake as a parent, your capacity to nurture is still yours to express. If you are a woman who is willing to find the roots of her low self-esteem after two marriages to abusive men, true love is still yours to find.

As Buddha once wrote, "You can search throughout

the entire universe for someone who is more deserving of your love and affection than you are yourself, and that person is not to be found anywhere. You yourself, as much as anybody in the entire universe deserve your love and affection."

Do not walk away from your gifts, thinking you have lost your claim to them. They remain yours to open. Forever.

ively—from my pain. And people looking to anes-
themselves are experts at finding accomplices to
rate a conspiracy of denial. They *have* to because
nderlying emotions are constantly threatening to
. They need a team to keep those emotions out of
usness.

ery may love company, but denial absolutely *re-*
.

k around you at the people you've attracted. They
omething inside you. Unless you're working for
y or a rehab clinic, you won't find yourself sur-
d by addicts if you aren't either an addict yourself
e very least, an enabler. You won't find yourself
ded by people who keep undermining you, unless
bt or dislike yourself. You won't find yourself sur-
d by people who keep asking way too much of you,
ou think your value is determined by how much
eed you. You won't find yourself surrounded by
ho live superficial lives filled with material things,
ou live your life the same way.

s a self-hating addict, desperately running from
, and I attracted people who disliked themselves
on the run, too. They valued me for my prob-
t my capacity to overcome them. And I valued
theirs. All of us unconsciously felt as though
ed each other to stay in numbing, escapist, self-

I Called You My Friends

T*here have been parts of* my life when I thought I had
a lot of friends, but the truth is, I've never had more than
a few genuine ones.

Looking back, I now realize that the periods during
which I believed I was surrounded by the most friends
were also the periods when I was furthest from my truth.
People thought I was a whole lot cooler back then—
during the 1980s and '90s—because I drank and used
drugs and surrounded myself with expensive toys. I mean,

I actually *owned* a DeLorean. That should tell you a lot about the drugs—not to mention what kind of person I saw myself as.

I laughed a fair amount and was good at getting my "friends" to laugh as well, even if it was usually at the expense of other people. I had a very good radar for what people truly valued in life or what they were sensitive about and I would needle them about it in a way that, at least to me, seemed like it was all in good fun. I assume if you asked the subjects of that needling, they may have interpreted it differently. But even when someone took offense, I could usually smooth things over with a nod or a wink. I could be charming when I wanted to be.

I know now that I was considered a good guy to hang around with back then because *I wasn't actually around at all.* I didn't disclose anything genuine about myself, other than sudden, destructive flashes of anger when someone pierced my emotional armor or challenged my authority. I didn't expect anyone else to share who he or she was inside, because I had no particular interest in that. To the contrary, I feared it. If someone wanted to connect *for real*, after all, I'd have to *be real* to do it.

I didn't expect anyone to back up his or her opinion with facts, because I was spouting my own opinions with no particular regard for them. I found that facts could actually get in the way of endless, circular arguments—

something I considered sport. I didn'[t]
to grapple with their own weaknesses,
run from my own. I'd just reassure t[hem]
would turn out fine, regardless of the[...]
people I hung out with that they jus[t ...]
the bright side" and tell nitpickers to [...]

What I really was to my "frien[ds ...]
ice-cold beer on a hot day. I didn't [...]
made them feel better for a little wh[ile ...]
24/7, with free entertainment. The [...]
tant rule of the house: Do not chall[enge ...]
dwell too much on yours. Come b[...]
shield and we'll all get along just fi[ne ...]

Sitting around a table and ta[lking ...]
been very much like sitting in a da[rk ...]
a movie about other people, munc[hing ...]
ing sodas. If anyone tried to spea[k ...]
real, like "Hey, I'm glad everybo[dy ...]
guess I'm distracted because my [...]
well . . ." then we'd just crack a f[...]
down lower, and crank up the vo[lume ...]

As I've said before, I attracte[d ...]
ever I went, coast to coast. I co[uld ...]
or Asia or Africa and found it, [...]
it because so many things I wa[...]
palpably designed around run[...]

defeating patterns of thought and behavior. It was as though we had tied our shoelaces together, yet kept wondering why we continually fell flat on our faces.

I lost my best friend in the world when I was thirteen—my mother. Until I fully grieved that loss, admitted how devastated I had been over her suicide, and forgave her (and myself) for it, I couldn't let anyone be my real friend. It just felt too risky. I was much more comfortable with people who couldn't care less about me or who secretly despised me. That way I could leave them or they could leave me without my heart breaking. They had no real power in my life because they had no real standing in my life.

Fortunately, I found Pat Gray, one of my very few true friends. He has told me he was drawn to me for a very different reason than my usefulness as an interpersonal anesthetic. He detected something kinder and gentler and much more vulnerable inside me than I was letting on, even to myself.

He didn't stay involved in my life over the years out of some pathological need to be needed; he stayed involved because he really loved something about me that I didn't even know was there (mainly because I was so intent on defending against it). Pat also saw my own capacity to love others, myself, and God long before I ever saw it. As he'd watch me struggling at work and at home, he'd keep saying, "Glenn, you're better than you think you are. Life isn't this tough. You're making it this way."

Precisely because Pat spouted New Age mumbo jumbo like that, I was very tough on him. I felt I had to keep him at a distance in order to keep my*self* at a distance. So I joked relentlessly about his PG-rated lifestyle. I joked about his religion. And yes, I even secretly wished that he would finally fall down and scrape his knees on the spiritual path he was traveling so that I would feel better about my own tortured, toxic journey.

What a friend I was.

Some part of me believed that if Pat kept navigating the twists and turns of life so elegantly, then sooner or later, I was going to have to admit that he really did have some answers I needed. A much bigger part of me didn't want those particular answers. I didn't want to have to stop using substances and money and anger to deaden my pain, and instead start exploring it. I mean, nobody *wants* pain (until you really think about the consequences of running from it). I didn't *want* to stop using my quick wit and sharp tongue to make a living and instead start using my heart and mind to *earn* one. That's so much more *effort*. I didn't want to let go of the inflated ego that protected and imprisoned my battered psyche and get anywhere near the exquisitely sensitive center of my soul.

But ultimately, thank God, I did anyway.

Pat stayed by my side through all of it. Even when he was living in another state, we were in touch every week and got together every few months. He was with me when I was making lots of money and living large and he was with me when I was broke and frightened and thinking I would be better off not living at all. He stayed with me when I fired a man for not handing me a Sharpie, and he was with me when firing someone over a pen was the last thing I'd ever do. Pat is still with me today, working by my side. If my business were to evaporate, if depression descended upon me, if I reached for a Jack and Coke and actually drained the glass, he would still be there. I just know it.

Do you have any idea what a gift it is to me to know that I am worthy of the unwavering support of someone who has his own life so put together?

God will put somebody near you who can be your genuine friend. That's because your true self—the really lovable and loving person you are at your core—is never completely extinguished, and someone, somewhere will resonate with that part of you. Please, don't be like me and keep that person (or, if you've hit the jackpot, those *people*) at a distance for decades.

Close your eyes right now, this very moment, and think whether you might have a friend like Pat, someone who sees through your shield into your core. Are they down the street, in the office next to yours, in the seat next to you as you carpool to work, in the city you left last year, or back in your hometown? If someone comes to mind, pick up the phone and call that person. Send an email. Write a note. Tell them the truth—that you were reading a book that describes friendship as a gift and that it made you think about him or her. If you're like I was, they'll probably think you're screwing with them first— but that's okay.

It might take two calls, or three, or five over time. It doesn't matter. Just think about Pat and me: I probably waited twenty years or so to tell him I loved him and would walk over hot coals for him if he needed me to.

But also consider whether *you* might be *someone else's* Pat. Are you the last hope for a friend who has given up on themselves? Have you given up on them, too?

Real friends have a unique power over each other. Their opinions matter; their words count. If a real friend says something to you then you take it to heart—which is precisely why people usually have so few real friends to begin with. Take Pat, for instance. If he disagrees with me, I have to really consider his perspective because I respect him and because he *knows* me. If I disappoint him through some fault of mine, it hurts me, because I believe I owe him my best. If he were to abandon me in a time of need or defraud me, it would cut me to the core, yet I would not abandon him if he wanted to make amends. If he were, God forbid, to die, I would suffer greatly. All of that makes me more vulnerable at the same time as it makes me stronger, and it has taken me most of my life to realize that those two things usually go together.

Once I learned the value of real friendship, I built my whole company and my whole life around it. My media business isn't just a collection of talented people. I have my friends with me at work. If I were to let them down by half-hearted effort, they'd call me on it. If I kept it up so long that their own talents were being wasted, they would leave, and be right to do so.

As I was writing these pages I made a call to Keith so that we could finally have a conversation that had taken us about five years to get to. I told him that working on this book had made me appreciate just how closely aligned our spirits were and that I looked forward to not only writing more together, but to our families spending even more time together.

He told me that he felt exactly the same way and that I had become an important part of his life and that he was very grateful for our friendship. He told me that he wanted his children to know mine and that our friendship had been helping his patients by adding another dimension to the way he went about trying to heal them.

My point is that friendships do not merely add together the gifts that God has given each individual: They multiply them through the immeasurable, miraculous force of spiritual synergy. In the case of true friendship, one plus one equals far more than two.

A real friendship is like a diamond. It doesn't degrade over time. It increases in value. Go and unearth any that have lingered just beneath the surface of your consciousness or even in the deeper recesses of your memory.

The word *friend* is mentioned ninety times in the Bible. We are told, "Genuine friends must be cherished and not forsaken." (Proverbs 27:10)

I know plenty about that now.

We are also told, "Faithful are the wounds of a friend; but the kisses of an enemy are deceitful." (Proverbs 27:6)

Sadly, I know plenty about that, too.

There had been people around me during much of my professional life whom I considered friends, but who were really emotional vampires. They were there simply in order to feast off my energy, like the promoter, manager, and cornermen of a boxer who is too old to be in the ring. I don't hate them, because vampires only do what comes naturally to them—feast on the life force of others. And hating them would only deplete me.

I knew these people were "friend vampires" because they were there for me when I was flush with cash and popularity and then—poof!—they disappeared the second

I sold my Mercedes and couldn't figure out how to pay six hundred dollars a month in rent. That happens. People get scared. I was actually too panicked and ashamed at the time to fully take notice. But, then, *presto!* These people reappeared when I got famous—not to reconnect for real, only to do the vampire thing again. They couldn't have been more obvious about it. And that crushed me.

It's human nature to try to keep everyone around you happy at any cost. It's hard to find people who really care about what's happening in your life. Sometimes it's even harder to hear their opinion about it. But it is so much better to know where you really stand with the people you trust. The kisses you receive from enemies are far more toxic than the wounds inflicted by friends.

I hope you never have to suffer the kind of collapse I did. But the upside of complete moral and financial Armageddon is that you get to see who your friends really are in clear view. Unless you're in the midst of your own Beck-style collapse, you'll just have to figure out who the real ones are while they remain in your life.

You can begin to do this by thinking about who among your "friends" has never disagreed with an opinion of yours, challenged you to try harder, think more deeply, or to abide by a higher moral code. If that brings someone to mind, either they're as uncomfortable with themselves as I was or they're a vampire friend just sapping your energy and providing nothing of value in return. Either way, they're not going to be there when you really need them.

One note of caution from my own experience, however: you can't fall into the trap of hating the people who let you down this way. Remember, no one becomes a false friend who hasn't learned toxic lessons in life and has yet to figure out how to *unlearn* them. Also remember that exercising compassion empowers you. Don't automatically write people off when they disappoint you, if they sincerely try to heal the rift they've created.

Believe me, I've needed that brand of compassion myself. My mentor is a man who is quite possibly the most honorable, caring, and compassionate person on earth. That man is Jon Huntsman, Sr., one of our nation's foremost business leaders and philanthropists. Jon has already given well over $1 billion to charity, and he has graced me personally with his time and wisdom and emotional support over the years. I can't overstate how much I respect him. I believe he is one of the finest people I will ever meet in this world—maybe *the* finest.

I tell you about him in the context of compassion because I once made a negative, offhanded comment about his son, Jon Huntsman, Jr., the current ambassador to China and former governor of Utah. I hadn't done my homework, and what I said was not only unfair to my friend, it turned out to be just plain *wrong*.

I got a note from Jon Sr. after my comment. It was honest and to the point. He told me how hurt he was that I would do harm to someone he loved. He told me that he thought he had opened his heart to me and treated me like family and that he was shocked and disappointed that I would betray his trust like that.

I wrote back to him and admitted that I had been wrong to comment on something I didn't have sufficient information about, especially when it concerned his son. I told him I wasn't perfect and that I would understand if he just couldn't bring himself to trust me again. I had brought it on myself as I had done so many times in my life.

It was the last thing I expected, but sending that note brought up feelings inside me from my mother's death. I began to cry, because I realized that I might once again be saying goodbye to another person who had believed in me.

Jon called me after he received my note. I tried to prepare for the worst—that I had so violated his trust that this would be our last call. I picked up the phone.

"Hi, Jon," I said.

"Hello, Glenn, I received your note."

"I know I hurt your son," I began. "I know there isn't any way to really make things right. But—"

"Now, wait a second," he said sternly.

This was all sounding very bad.

"Did you mean what you said in that note about not even having really researched what you commented on, to my son's detriment?"

Uh-oh. "Yes," I said.

"So you literally did what you did out of carelessness?"

"Listen, I have nothing to argue with you . . ."

"And then you wrote a note and asked me to wipe the slate clean?"

"I thought maybe with time, maybe after a while . . ."

"Then I guess that's all the business we have."

My heart fell.

"We're good with each other," he went on. "Of course I forgive you. I love you, Glenn. You should know that by now. Everyone makes mistakes."

My eyes were closed, and I spoke very quietly, because I knew I was in the presence of greatness. "Thank you, Jon," I said. "I mean, I don't know *how* to thank you."

"Keep being my brother," he said.

I have seen my share of challenges in life. No doubt more are on the way. But I now have friends by my side who know exactly who I really am. That means I can weather storms that might otherwise have the force to cut me down. And that knowledge comforts, sustains, and strengthens me every day.

Whatever troubles you will be so much easier to face

with true friends by your side and so much harder to over-come without them (or worse, with vampire friends). So take an inventory of your relationships and then turn on your computer. Take out your pen. Write to a real friend. Tell that person who he or she is in your life—even if you've waited years to say it. Tell them that you are ready to make some important changes in your life and that you want—no, you *need*—them to be along with you for the journey.

KEITH

The Fifth Wonder: Friendship

Friendship is one of those things in life that most people tend to feel, without wanting to look at it too deeply. Maybe we fear that in examining it too closely we will dissect away its magic.

Nothing could be further from the truth. Much like love or courage or faith or compassion or truth, friendship is an irreducible human experience. It isn't something that can be explained away or reduced to its molecular structure or summed up in a series of chemical equations or mathematical calculations. You'll never find it on an MRI. Peel back layer upon layer of the forces that coalesce into a friendship, and you will find immeasurable, inexplicable energy that I believe comes directly from the synergy of two utterly unique personalities.

Having at least one true friend in the world is like having a refuge from the tides of everyday life that might otherwise sweep you out to sea. A friend can anchor you by giving you perspective that fully incorporates who you are as a person and what ideas you hold dear, but is one step removed from your own anxiety or anger or excitement.

True friends can operate almost in tandem, intellectually and emotionally. They feel safe enough with one another to borrow the best qualities and skills that each possesses.

Whether you are faced with surviving the loss of a loved one or a financial reversal or a medical illness or even the toll of social and political upheaval on your family, having one friend in the world who understands you and loves you and will do what he or she can to help you will fortify your spirit in dramatic ways. Two people standing against the tide are not twice as strong, they are exponentially as strong. This is because their combined strength includes not only their mass and musculature, but also their ability to inspire one another to reach deeper for the resolve to stay on their feet and actually move in the direction one of them really wants or needs to go.

It is a thousand times harder to bully a person with a true friend than it is to bully a person who feels completely alone in the world. The force of friendship, then, is no less a miracle of nature than the wind or the force of gravity or fusion. It is energy from God meant to help you live a powerful life.

Finding true friends in life has much in common with finding your true path. There are almost always false starts. Most of us have suffered through false "friends"— maybe you have such a person in your life right now. And you may well come upon more of them. But if that were to dissuade you from being open to the miracle of *genuine friendship*, then you would be denying yourself one of life's true miracles.

A true friend will often appear, almost magically, at the time you most need them—especially when you begin to discover and develop the other wonders we describe in this book. That's because the other wonders help you become your*self*, and only when you are a genuine individual can you be available for a genuine relationship of any kind, including friendship.

Remember, any false friends you have (or have had) were *attracted to you for a reason*—because of your unwillingness or inability to follow the bread crumbs and find your true path. As Glenn discovered, false friends become painfully obvious when you begin being honest with yourself.

You have this book in your hands *now*. Now is the time to be alert to welcoming a true friend into your heart.

That person, like Pat in Glenn's life, may be someone you already know, but someone you are purposefully keeping at a distance. You are intent on not trusting anyone or letting anyone really get to know you because you're worried that their trust or friendship will ultimately be broken.

While you're free to go through life that way—and many people do—it's not easy. Friends help level out our highs and lows and keep it all in perspective. But how do you go about recognizing a true friend? It's not easy, so I've created something called the *Five Ways to True Friendship*, in order to help. These are by no means the only ways true friends can show their authenticity, but most true friends usually demonstrate at least two of these qualities.

1. *A True Friend Will Share Her Pain With You, Not Just Her Triumphs*

People don't really bond around the highlights of their résumés, the awards they've won, the way they've remodeled their kitchen, their kids' accomplishments, getting a raise at work, or getting engaged. Those things are easy to talk about with anyone. They feel good to talk about. People bond when they allow others to know what *hasn't* gone well in their lives or what is not currently going well. They bond when they take chances and reveal their weaknesses and disappointments and struggles and fears to one another. They bond when they summon the courage and faith to tell the truth about their lives and kindle each other's compassion.

Courage, faith, truth, compassion, and friendship all work together in life.

A person capable of true friendship needs real support and is willing to take a risk to find it. Such a person might tell you about a business that has gone badly or a pregnancy that has gone awry or a romantic relationship that was painful or childhood events that were traumatic.

Be on the lookout for those who have a genuine desire for intimacy and support and the ability to voice those needs. If such individuals are already in your life, then you may be fortunate to have true friends already. But if you meet such people, resist putting up your own shields and dismissing them automatically as needy or dramatic. Start to wonder, instead, whether they might simply be unafraid of being honest. *Listen* to them.

2. *Monitor How You Feel When Telling Someone Your Own Life Story or While Sharing Chapters of It as They Unfold*

Someone who is sincerely interested in you will want to make sure they really understand you. So, they'll have questions for you. They may ask you to repeat something to see if they heard you correctly. Or they might ask for more detail about something you describe. Don't be surprised if you get an email after a lunch together saying, "Wait, I was thinking about what you said about your marriage and I don't know if I got the whole picture when you told me he was irresponsible at times. In what way? When?"

See, true friends don't simply take things at face value. Because they *really* value you, a true friend will press you for your truth, even at the risk of getting you angry, and you'll *feel* it.

"I don't know if I believe what you just said," a true friend might tell you, "and I don't know if *you* really believe it."

Or, "I see you going to work at your business, but I don't see you *working* your business."

Or, "You say you want to lose weight, but you won't go to the gym with me, and I've asked a dozen times."

Or, "You say you're getting serious about putting away money to go back to school, but you're looking at a new car when yours runs fine."

You get the point.

If you've never felt pressed to say what you really think or to do what you really dream of doing by someone who says they're your friend, then it's worth spending some time thinking about whether they really are. On the other hand, if you have distanced yourself from someone who *did* press you in those ways, then reach out to them today and think about bringing them into your life in a more meaningful way.

3. *Look for Those Who Urge You to Honor Yourself by Having Good Values*

It's so common for folks who are toying with the idea of violating their core beliefs to first share the thought with others, almost as a request for support. You may have done it yourself, bouncing the idea off a "friend" of calling in sick to work when you're not, or canceling an appointment for the second time with someone who has asked for your advice, or "trying to hide" a little income here or there, or keeping a secret about one of your kids from your spouse.

A true friend is one who will object and tell you, as Pat once told Glenn, "You're a better person than that."

Ultimately, true friends see your potential, often more clearly than you do. That's a big reason why they are able to so dramatically increase your positive energy.

Here's a metaphor: just about everyone has had the experience of putting on a dress or a suit and then stepping in front of a mirror and saying to someone, "How do I look?"

The reason you ask that question is that you can't be entirely certain yourself. You need another set of eyes, because yours could be deceiving you. It gives you confidence to have another trusted opinion. It can literally change the way you *wear* those clothes. You feel differently, more self-confident, because you are not alone in the crowd.

Well, guess what? You need someone by your side who will tell you how you look intellectually and physically and morally and ethically and emotionally. Moreover, you deserve that person. Everyone does.

A person with no genuine friends cannot walk their path toward truth. Isolation is just too great a burden—and it's *supposed* to be. We are meant to interact with others on a deep level, and beneath the surface, all of us appreciate others defending our values and principles even when we are willing to compromise them.

4. *Determine Whether a Friend Really Matters to You*

Even when Glenn was running as fast as he could from his truth, Pat's criticism of him for firing the man who had handed him the wrong kind of pen hit him hard. He *felt* as though he had fallen short. That's because the mirror reflecting how he "looked" ethically and emotionally— Pat's honest, loving assessment of him—was showing him how distorted he was from his ideal self. He tried to shake off that glimpse of himself in Pat's eyes, but he never forgot it.

You'll remember that when Glenn was headed to get even with the person who had insisted he pay back every dollar owed to him right on time, Tania was a true friend. She asked Glenn questions that were uncomfortable about why he was doing what he was doing. She got to the bottom of the fact that his motivation was retribution. She helped him decide for himself whether that was really in character for him and a reflection of the best he could be. She acted as a mirror so that Glenn could see that the drive he was taking in order to get even was taking him away from his emotional and ethical and moral core. She showed him so he could see how his rage had distorted him. And Glenn *felt* it. It *mattered* to him what Tania thought, so he turned the car around.

More than twenty years ago, I was in psychotherapy with the late psychiatrist James Mann, then eighty. I knew from the first minutes of my first visit with him that I was in the presence of a person who could become a true friend.

Mann, wearing a seersucker suit with an open-collar shirt, his hair gray and unruly, was sitting in a deep, upholstered armchair in his study. I was in a matching armchair about six feet away. Mann sat silently for a minute, staring at me, then out the window to his yard, then back again, seeing if I would begin the conversation. There was only silence. He smiled, finally, and said, "Okay, I'll start. What have you come here to talk about?"

I wasn't certain how quickly or thoroughly I wanted to address what was really bothering me: the death of a fellow psychiatry resident in my training program, together with feelings that the depression I had confronted in medical school might be coming back. "I can't say I have anything earth-shattering," I hedged. "It's mostly that I haven't been in therapy at all yet, and I'm chief resident at Tufts, so my professors thought it would be an important experience."

"It could be," Mann said. "Or not. I've seen it go both ways."

"Right . . . ," I said, a little taken aback. "Well, I could use some help, I think, figuring out a few thoughts I have about life, maybe going over my relationship with my girl-friend and the way—"

Mann held up a hand that stopped me in midsentence. "Do you ever get the sense as you're talking," he said, "that you're completely full of crap?"

I laughed, but only for a moment, because I saw that Mann was barely grinning. Then I took a deep breath and let it out. I felt precisely what you should feel when you're in the presence of someone who might be a true friend—the uncompromising but warm intention of a person who sincerely wants to know the *real* you. "Sometimes," I replied. "Yes, sometimes I do."

Mann smiled. I remember it to this day as one of the most loving smiles I have ever seen. A father's smile. "Well, here's the thing," Mann said. "It's your time, and it's your money, but most importantly, it's your life. If you insist on wasting all three, I'm going to sit here with you anyhow. We could be at it for months. But I hope to the bottom of my heart that that doesn't happen."

"I don't want to waste my life," I responded immediately. "I just lost a friend of mine just a year older than

I am who I really cared about. I don't want to waste a minute."

"Now you're talking," Mann said. "Tell me all about him."

You can sometimes recognize people who have the capacity to truly care about you from the first time you meet them. And when that happens, it's possible you've met a true friend. Remember, there are no coincidences in life.

5. *Stop Fooling Yourself into Thinking That You Are with True Friends if You Aren't*

False friends are just another drug. They not only fail to tap into your genuine thoughts and feelings, they also reinforce your habit of maintaining distance from them. That's why it is literally better to "detox" from false friends and spend time alone than to bide your time with them for fear of being isolated. When you say goodbye to anything or anyone toxic, you are telling yourself that you are worthy of so much more.

When it's all said and done, true friendships bring us closer to happiness by forcing us to be our best, and by challenging us when we're not. And if you're wondering who in your past or present may qualify, try testing them against this timeless quote from Walter Winchell:

A real friend is one who walks in when the rest of the world walks out.

Pat and Tania met that standard for Glenn. Which friends meet it for you?

GLENN

Isn't It My Life, Period?

By now, *you probably know* a fair amount about me. Parts of my life have caused me and others a good deal of pain. I emerged from those chapters with the determination to pursue my truth. I didn't have much choice, frankly. It was either that or die. I know God *meant* for me to choose. I don't think I ever would have, otherwise, and I know for a fact that I never would have truly lived.

I now strive to include in my life only those ideas and people and plans that resonate deeply with me and seem consistent with what God wants for me and from me. I believe to the core of my being that meditating on the name of God—*I AM*, or *He Who Is Ever Becoming What He Is*—helps remind me that I have a spiritual obligation to be genuine. I refuse to pretend to be someone I am not. I have traveled too far to let that happen. I have hurt too much and hurt too many people to let it happen.

I want the same thing for you. So does Keith. That's the whole reason we're writing this book. We want you to let go of the false support you may be clinging to from those who have made you believe that there's no safety net below. We want you to experience the joy and empowerment that comes when you release your grip and land safely on firm ground, facing your true path.

We want you to become what you were meant to be from the beginning of time.

I have found that big questions are important to ask, because they're the only ones that have a chance of yielding big answers. So let me ask you one: if you and I each have the right and the obligation to live a life that is true to our*selves*, then how do we balance our needs and callings with the claims that others have on us? How do we move confidently in the direction of who we really are when we are already connected to other people who may not like that idea very much? Can we simply be rid of them if they don't accept or don't seem to *fit* with our newly discovered, truer selves?

If I had a friend and was to realize that he had always encouraged me to be dependent on him and had never urged me to stand on my own two feet, would I be free to end our relationship when I became stronger and more independent? What if instead of being a friend that person was my brother? What if it was my wife?

If I were a partner in a business that was struggling to survive in turbulent times, and the pressure made me realize that I truly wanted to become a teacher, would I have license to leave that very day to pursue my calling? Would it be a lie to stay one more moment at my desk, pretending to be committed to the venture at hand?

Put even more simply: *Isn't it my life, period? Doesn't that leave me entirely free?*

You will have to come to your own determination, but for me, the answer to the first question is *yes*, and the second is *no*.

It took me some time to figure out that my authenticity was, is, and always will comprise more than my current goals, opinions, and feelings—however heartfelt. My authenticity also includes covenants I have made with others and with God.

That's right, covenants. These are sacred promises

that are as much a part of me as my DNA and are, in the case of my blood relatives, literally entwined with it. To violate them would be to violate my*self.*

So, *yes*, it is my life, period. But, *no*, that doesn't leave me entirely free of responsibility to others. What sort of life would that be anyway? Who would want to lead such a life—free not only to triumph alone and celebrate alone, but also to fail alone and suffer alone?

I have a covenant with my father. It binds us together and obligates me to understand him and help him understand me and use my mind and spirit to heal our relationship to whatever extent I can.

I have a continuing covenant with my mother, even though she has departed. It obligates me to understand her struggles and her suicide and use the insight and wisdom I gain to improve my life and the lives of my descendants.

I have covenants with my sisters to be a reservoir of memory for them about what we experienced together as children and to be a person in this world they can call upon for help at any time.

I have a covenant with my wife to create a family that will nurture our souls and those of our children, our parents, and all those who come to be connected to us. That includes my friends, my business partners, and my employees.

I have covenants with my children to love them, guide them, and help them live the lives they were meant to live.

I have covenants with my grandparents. In coming to understand their strengths and limitations, I can learn something about the roots of my own strengths and limitations, and those of my children, and their children.

What my father experienced with his father is not only inscribed between the lines of my life story, but plays as music in the background of my children's life stories as well. And it will, though perhaps more faintly, still play in the background of my grandchildren's.

I have covenants with my friends, employees, and business partners to not leave them in any kind of bad situation, even if I *do* leave them, in time, to pursue my personal truth.

I have a covenant with my country to do what I believe will keep it strong and true, even if that means deferring cherished goals of mine that beckon me in other directions.

It is my life. Entirely. Absolutely. But to ignore my covenants with others would be to ignore God and dishonor that life. I choose not to diminish my*self* that way.

I am not at liberty to drink again. I don't have the *right*. It would hurt me, but it would also do harm to my family, friends, business partners, and causes I care deeply about. I am not at liberty to do drugs. It would hurt me, but it could shatter my children's sense of security and my wife's respect for me and my partners' confidence in the future of our work together. I am not at liberty to ruin my body with cigarettes or to let myself grow (too) obese or to ignore the advice of my eye doctor and accelerate the loss of my vision. Those things would hurt me, but they would cheat others of the covenants I have made with them. I am not even at liberty to keep an idea of mine to myself if I believe it can illuminate an important issue or encourage people to live lives based on purpose and meaning.

I do not believe I am free (and do not wish to be free) to think of myself as newly sprung to the planet, as a "Platonic conception of myself," as Jay Gatsby saw himself in *The Great Gatsby*. I was not free to ignore my covenants even as I reformatted the hard drive of my soul. I am the product of many other lives, and to deny this would be to deny my bond with the eternal, immeasurable connections that fill me with a sense of meaning, responsibility, and destiny.

Just as important, denying my covenants would deny me the essential opportunity to continue remaking myself. Because part of my true path in this life is to identify, understand, and heal the broken elements of my relationships, thereby also healing what is broken inside me. If I can find the courage to feel the pain I experienced as a child, have faith that the pain will strengthen me, summon the determination to unearth and embrace my truth, and find the compassion to forgive those who have harmed me, then I am serving my best self, not diminishing it. I am then truly respecting my birthright as a "temple of God."

These concepts ring true regardless of what point of view you approach life from. My father did not become my father by accident. My mother did not become my mother by accident. They were alive on the planet at the same time and found one another partly in order to begin my journey here. And since their union was no coincidence, my journey includes, and will always include, understanding myself in the context of my connection to each of them. And for the rest of the days we share, I will also be helping my father understand himself through my evolving relationship with him.

I am my father's son and my father's father.

If I really did have a brother who had fostered my dependency on him, part of our journey here together on the planet would almost certainly be for me to claim my autonomy without hating him or forsaking him. That might well allow him to realize that living my own life had not ultimately weakened him, but in fact had empowered him to live his own life, too. He would be free of the burden of believing—wrongly—that he needed to protect me. By honoring our covenant, while honoring my*self*, I would have helped to heal us both.

The fact that I am always attempting to honor my truth doesn't release me from my covenant to honor my wife, even if we find ourselves in conflict. The conflict itself is meant to be. It is an opportunity to grow. Our marriage is no accident. It is the crucible in which we have the chance to help one another find our best selves, walk our true paths, and help create other human beings who can travel even further, see even more clearly, and show their own love of God.

You have covenants, too. And you know in your heart what they are. Try to deny them and, far from liberating yourself, you will only diminish yourself.

See, I realized through experience that covenants are just another kind of truth. Keeping them can be very difficult and very painful but that's exactly how it's *supposed* to be. Everything in life that we continue to embrace and refine is arduous. Editing a story to bring out the deep character of each person in it is a lot harder than just throwing the pages away and starting over. Putting the fifth layer of paint on a canvas requires respect for all four layers that came before it. It's a lot harder than pulling out a blank canvas and beginning to execute another vision. Winning the peace is usually much harder than winning the war.

Well, guess what? Parenting a teenager is usually a lot tougher than parenting a six-year-old. Maintaining intimacy and communication in a marriage of twenty years is usually a lot tougher than in a marriage of two years. Keeping a genuine friend for life is a lot tougher than finding someone new to hang out with every couple of years.

Keeping covenants requires much more than just keeping my word. I could do that passively, even while filled with resentment. I serve my covenants actively in order to stay on the path I was meant to travel, even when the terrain is challenging, even when massive obstacles must be removed in order to see just a few feet ahead.

I have to be dedicated to putting that fifth layer of paint on the canvases of my relationships in order to bring them to "the next level," or to attempt to correct an unfortunate perspective that damages the whole.

There is a difference, however, between the act of keeping a covenant when there is the real possibility of doing so, and the act of remaining in an orbit that is depleting and limiting you and cannot be changed—no matter what. In other words, there are indeed times in life when you may need, after careful consideration and much effort, to move on from promises you have made. That may include:

- Instances when you are, for all intents and purposes, not the same person who made the covenants in the first place; and
- Your new defining qualities are utterly unacceptable to someone with whom you are connected; and
- You have tried, in a fair and reasonable way, to alter the "terms" of your connection, in order to do no harm.

All three of these statements would have to be true in order for me to exercise my freedom and move on from my covenant.

For example, let's say that you decided that your career as an investment banker is strangling you and that you have to pursue your real dream of becoming an architect. You shared this realization with your wife and listened to her concerns about the financial impact on your family of such a decision. You have, therefore, come up with the idea of beginning your schooling slowly, part-time, a few nights a week. Your sleep will suffer, and, sure, maybe there won't be a family trip this year, but you won't be selling your house or being absent from home.

What you hear back from your wife, however, is that there isn't any leeway at all; she believes that life isn't about "dreams," that you just have to keep on keeping on, and that all this talk about "becoming the person you were meant to be" is for people who don't have careers already. She suggests you should explain away whatever you think is in your heart as a midlife crisis and let it go at that.

You convince your wife to try marriage counseling. But the upshot is that she has always thought of you as self-focused, to the exclusion of those around you, and that your latest goal is more of the same. You figure she may have a point, so you ask her how you could pursue your goal while keeping your covenants to her and your children. And you hear back that the well is dry; there's no way she can support your ambition at all. She doesn't believe you when you say that it's the career you dreamed about as a kid and have to devote yourself to before your death. She says if you want to start acting like a grad student at forty years old you can do it on your own.

Maybe you try to let your dream go and you just can't. You believe—at the core of your being—that you were *meant* to design buildings and that you can *contribute* something special doing it. You don't want your kids growing up seeing their father working only in hopes of getting rich; you want them to see you working in hopes of creating something extraordinary that stands the test of time.

Then, my friend, you may have to leave. If you were to do so, you would have to do it responsibly and with as much love for all concerned—including your wife—as humanly possible. But your love for self would have to be served.

Are you surprised to hear me say that? Does that sound like violating a covenant? It isn't. Covenants are, by their nature, sacred agreements between two or more parties. If you promised to stay married to someone who would love you forever, then realize you are not loved at all by that person, and that there is no reasonable hope that you ever will be, and that the example of your broken relationship is a burden to your children, then you must accept this reality: There is no covenant. There is only your truth. And in the end, the truth always wins.

Covenants are not contracts that include your spiritual destruction. God would never ask that of you nor want that for you. He wants you to have your moment. At the same time, a change in plans doesn't mean a covenant has to be broken.

More than anything else, use common sense. Respect and honor the covenants and promises you've made, and use every bit of intellect and insight and determination you can summon to keep them. But don't deny reality if what you thought was a lifelong obligation degenerates into a contract that includes your spiritual destruction. That's the time to remind yourself that sometimes you have to risk the life you're currently living to instead live the one that God needs you to.

KEITH

The Sixth Wonder: Family

Of all the covenants in your life, those with your wife and your children are the most powerful. Becoming the person you were meant to be and clearing any hurdles in your way will be infinitely easier if you understand and optimize the powerful emotional and spiritual bonds that link you together.

Your family relationships are, in fact, bread crumbs leading you to your true path. They are challenges that help make you the most complete, loving person you can be.

Thinking about family relationships as challenges may not seem all that appealing, but if you really focus on all the highs and lows of being a brother or sister or son or daughter or husband or wife or father or mother, then you might not object. Almost all such relationships course through good times and bad times, if for no other reason than that family members are generally around one another so much. The extensive exposure dissolves the niceties and posturing often present in relationships with colleagues or friends. You see each other when you're happy and sad, rested and tired, patient and irritable, funny and just plain annoying.

And that's only the beginning of the challenges. There's also the sense of loss we carry deep within us for the perfect family relationships we once hoped for. As children, we are available for ideal parenting, but we meet up with our flawed fathers and mothers who *inevitably* love us imperfectly, burdened as they are with the legacies of their own disappointments and fears and traumas. We hope for perfect camaraderie with our brothers or sisters, but encounter sibling rivalry. We marry in hope that bliss will last a lifetime, but run into those moments we feel misunderstood, forgotten, or jealous. We have children whom we love endlessly, yet we also experience conflicts between nurturing them and setting limits for them, supporting them and giving them independence, investing our time in them as parents and giving ourselves enough time to grow as individuals.

The complexities of these dynamics are like tangles or knots in magical strings connecting you to your family members. Untangling the strings yields a stronger safety net for you and for them than anyone in the family could have imagined without making the effort. But the struggle to get everything straight and true also has another benefit: it helps you express parts of yourself that you might never have otherwise discovered.

No one asks for challenges. Certainly, we would be tempted to edit out the really difficult pages of our childhoods and married lives if we had the choice. But we don't have that choice. We can only serve our*selves* and God by not running from those pages, and instead seeking to understand every lesson meant for us within them, thereby turning our lives and the lives of our families into stories of courage, faith, truth, and compassion.

Besides, think of the dangers we'd face should we be able to edit out the difficulties we encounter in our families. Would perfect harmony really create children who struggle to find themselves and express themselves, even when they encounter hurdles in the outside world? Would they ever really be able to say "This is who I am and I will not yield" if they didn't struggle for autonomy at home first? Would people really be better off marrying partners who do not trigger in them core issues that remain unresolved from childhood, thereby offering them the opportunity to finally overcome them?

One of my former patients was a fifty-five-year-old man I'll call James. He managed a hedge fund and was regarded as an extremely strong leader and risk taker. James had profited greatly from relying on his "gut feelings," which often ran counter to the prevailing wisdom. The dozens of employees who reported to him revered him as a genius. They tried to mimic his trading strategies as closely as possible and often made themselves and the firm a lot of money in the process.

The problem was that things had become much harder for James to manage at home. His wife, Ellen, thirty-eight, was talking about filing for divorce. She had chosen to spend her time raising the couple's three children. Now, with the children in school full-time, she was much less busy and wanted to express parts of herself that she had put on hold—including ideas she had about starting a business of her own. She wanted to share more of her thoughts and feelings about her career plans with James and had said she needed more of his time. But he hadn't reacted in a way that satisfied her.

"Maybe I'm just too much of a pragmatist," James told me, "but I don't see how my wife starting an interior design business makes a lot of sense. I mean, even if she were successful, we're talking about a fraction of my income."

I couldn't help but notice James's imperial tone, his regal salt-and-pepper hair, the monogram embroidered on one cuff of his shirt, his perfectly tailored suit. Everything about him spoke of perfection and control. "Does she say she wants to contribute to the family fortune or that she wants to express herself creatively?" I asked him.

James smiled. "Understood. No, she's not trying to be the breadwinner in the family. But look, over the past year, she's lurched from wanting to open a restaurant, to wanting to go back to school for a degree in international relations, to wanting to adopt another child, to wanting to open a yoga studio, now to this idea about interior decorating."

"That bothers you."

"Sure it does."

"Why? It certainly doesn't sound like she's under any financial pressure to make a choice and get going."

"It's just not the way I see the world. As far as I'm concerned, you make a plan and you execute it. Easy. Done."

"Like a stock trade," I said with a smile.

James laughed. "I'm a logical man. If my wife had stuck with her first idea or her second idea, I might have been more curious about one of them. But her fifth idea?" He shrugged. "Sorry, not so much."

"I get it," I said. "I know you're describing someone who's had a bunch of plans. And now you question how much she really cares about pursuing any of them. But wouldn't that be expected, since she's been raising the children for the past fifteen years?"

"Expected . . . I guess. Sure. But, see, I didn't expect *any* of this. When I married her she was very happy for me to go out there and handle the financial side of our lives while she took care of the home front. Now, when I can really consider putting my business in the hands of other people and traveling more, she wants to start decorating other people's houses and expressing herself. It's all mixed up. It makes no sense. My father had a saying: "When you have three ideas, it's probably because you don't have a single decent one.""

As you know, I believe a good deal of the help that psychiatrists offer people relates to their using a "third ear"—that inner monitoring of themselves while listening to patients that allows them not to dismiss something that doesn't sit entirely well with them. James quoting his father triggered my third ear. "Why did your father say that?" I asked.

"Why?" James replied.

"Yes. I mean, what led him to say it. Why did he tell you that? And when?"

"Why did he tell me that?" James repeated, almost as if stalling. He shrugged.

I waited.

"Well, I mean, I couldn't swear that those were his exact words. What he was getting at was that you don't get anywhere by being a dilettante—a dabbler."

"That's not how you remembered what he said, though," I countered. "The way you quoted him, he was suggesting that people who have more than a single, focused idea are *all* dilettantes. None of them are out there searching or just plain *full* of good ideas." I paused. "Do you agree with him?"

James shifted in his seat. "I suppose not—not when you put it that way."

"I wonder why did he feel the need to tell you that? Were you unfocused during part of your life?"

"I wouldn't have dared," James said, immediately, almost automatically. He shook his head, as if trying to shake off the impact of his words. Then he tried to run away from the whole discussion. "With all due respect, I really don't know where this is going. I'm trying to save my marriage today, and we're going all the way back to when I was nineteen or something. My dad's been gone over a decade now."

James wasn't comfortable when he didn't know *where things were going*. That was one of the reasons he was in my office to begin with. "Trust me, this may feel like a detour, but I promise, it's not. Tell me about your dad. He was . . . what—demanding?"

"Let's just put it this way: my father was a worrier. Back then, he wanted the best for me and he worried I wouldn't amount to anything."

"When you were nineteen?"

"You don't give up."

"Nope."

"I wanted to leave college for a year. My father said, 'Fine, but then you're not coming back home and you're not getting a dollar from me or your mother.' He didn't speak to me until I told him I'd stay put. The tough-love thing."

"A little heavy on the tough, a little light on the love, if you ask me."

James nodded. A bit of his brashness seemed to leave him. "I can't disagree there."

"So what happened?"

"I stayed in college, finished my degree in economics and applied math, and the rest is history. It worked out pretty well, I'd say."

"Seems so. You got rich, anyhow, right? Just out of curiosity, though, what was it that you were going to leave school to do?"

"I really didn't know," he said. "I had a bunch of . . ." He stopped himself.

"A bunch of ideas?" I asked. "Maybe, say, *five*?"

We looked at one another, then smiled together.

"Here's the thing," I said. "If you grow up with a father who's so anxious about whether you'll be a success that he tells you he's through with you if you start looking anywhere but straight ahead, then you can end up linking love and support with never changing your mind or your plans. And that could leave you in a mess of trouble when you try to understand a woman who's raised her children and wants to remake part of her life. Because if she's not too damaged, she's going to go searching, no matter what you tell her. And that could leave you on the edge of divorce. The truth is, your father probably wouldn't have stopped being your father if you insisted on that year off from college. Your wife, on the other hand, could actually stop being your wife if you insist she look straight ahead and stop trying to share her ideas with you."

"You're saying I won't listen to Ellen because my dad wouldn't listen to me."

"I'm sure there's more to it than that, but it sounds like that's part of it. If you *had* listened to her, if you had shown her the kind of love and support you might have hoped for from your father at one time, then you would have had to think again about what he wasn't able to provide you."

"I don't want to paint him as a villain, because he wasn't. He did a lot for me."

"I don't see him as a villain. I see him as a man who

probably had great strengths and some limitations, like a lot of people. Whatever the limitations were, and wherever they came from, they injured you. But they weren't so dark that they prevented you from trying to understand your wife by coming to see a psychiatrist. Your dad never did close your mind to other perspectives and possibilities."

"You wanna tell my wife that?" James asked.

I smiled.

"No, I mean it, can I bring her here to talk to you? Can we come as a couple?"

"On one condition," I said.

"Shoot."

"Before you go home tonight, stop by a bookstore, pick up a book on interior design, and give it to her."

"It's as easy as that, huh?" James asked.

"Let's be honest. If it were that easy, you'd have done it months ago, and you wouldn't need me."

"Okay. Fair enough. I'll do it."

James took home a book on interior design that evening. He phoned me the next day and told me that it had obviously taken his wife a little by surprise. "She wanted to know why I would all of a sudden be listening to her, so I told her the truth. I said I had listened to a psychiatrist that I'd met with and that I wanted her to meet you, too. She said she would."

"Great."

"I went a little further than you suggested with this whole 'new me' thing, by the way," James said.

"You bought two books?" I joked.

"I told her about my dad. I told her how I wanted that year to myself and I never took it and that maybe I was mixed up about tough love being the way to go."

"That's not a *little* further. That's a lot further. Good work."

"One thing I know is how to execute," James said. "When I see a trade worth making, I make it."

James and Ellen came to see me about a week later. It was obvious from the beginning of the session that there was more distance between the two of them than a book—or even two books—could bridge. Ellen sat rather stiffly, with her hands folded in her lap. She was a very pretty woman with long, straight blond hair. Her eyes never really wandered to her husband.

"I came today because James asked me to," Ellen said. "And I really appreciate you being available to see us. But even though James has been . . . well . . . different, since the two of you met, that doesn't change the fact that I think it's best that we think about ending things."

The words *think about ending things* gave me reason to believe that Ellen wasn't resolute about it. Her presence at the session was also encouraging. "You think you might want to move on," I said.

"I think that's just insane," James said.

Ellen glanced at him, shook her head, then looked back at me. "We aren't one month or one year into this problem," she said. "I've *lived* this problem with him for most of our marriage. James is very black-and-white. He wants everything stated in ten words or less, or his attention wanders to something else. And he never, never was concerned with my development as a person."

"You wanted to stay home to take care of the kids," James said, looking at me instead of his wife.

"It was never discussed," Ellen said. "It was assumed."

"Look, I made a mistake," James said. "Now I get it. You want something different."

"It's a little late, don't you think?" Ellen said, looking at him.

"I'm just wondering," I said. "Did you protest? Did you tell James how unfulfilled you felt?"

Ellen turned to me. "I should have to protest? How was I supposed to do that? I left home at twenty-one to marry Jim. I commuted to college. I'm not saying I would have done anything differently, but I would have liked the opportunity to *decide*. And I would have hoped my husband would at least *listen* to me when I finally did get around to thinking about other ways to express myself once the kids were older. My parents didn't exactly instill independence or confidence in me. They were old-school."

"Meaning?" I asked.

"Get married and have someone take care of you," she said.

"You bought that," I said with a grin.

"Hook, line, and sinker," Ellen said.

"Yeah, well, guess what?" I said, nodding over at James. "So did he."

Ellen glanced at James, and found him already looking at her. It took a few seconds for Ellen to look away, back at me. When she did, her eyes were less angry. "So all these years, he just sweeps under the carpet because we both *misunderstood* what a marriage should be?"

"If you were to sweep them under the carpet, you wouldn't have the chance to teach each other what marriage can *really* be, starting now," I replied.

Ellen sighed and shook her head. "And how exactly are we supposed to do that?"

I smiled, more to myself than anyone else. So many momentous changes in life begin with doubt that they can happen at all. "We're starting right now," I said. "Why don't you tell James how it *felt* when he wouldn't listen to you."

Ellen and James eventually decided to stay together. They were able to see, ultimately, that their marriage held the seeds of continued growth for each of them. Negative lessons they had learned in their families were actually part of what had brought them together; they were mirror images of one another. But inherent in them being a lock-and-key fit for one another's limitations, they had all they needed to open a new door and start a new chapter in their lives together.

Ellen actually went ahead and built her interior design business. James supported her decision and took an active interest in her work. He didn't try to control the business she was creating; he tried to understand and celebrate it.

A few years later, James called me to tell him about another wrinkle in the couple's relationship.

"She's got this business of hers really moving now," James said. "I'm proud of her."

"Not like a parent, I hope," I said. "Like a husband . . ."

"Absolutely."

"Sounds good to me."

"So, the thing is, I want to come back in and spend some more time talking."

"About?"

"Me, of course," James laughed. "Ellen brought up a kind of loose end in all this the other day."

"What was that?"

"Well, I never really did have that year to figure out what I wanted to do—who I wanted to *be*."

"And you're thinking maybe it's time to start figuring it out now," I said.

"Way past due. I'm a very, very good trader," James said. "But I'm not sure I'm *supposed* to be one at all. Does that sound nuts?"

"Not in the least."

"So we can figure out what I'm really meant to do? It's not too late?"

"You know it isn't, or you wouldn't be calling me," I said. "How does tomorrow look for you?"

The story of James and Ellen is, ultimately, a story about family. It is a story about the way that two people—in this case a husband and wife—can use their hearts and minds to trace the roots of the challenges they face in loving one another and find parts of themselves that they had left behind. It is a story about the way that untangling the strings connecting a couple, rather than severing them, can reveal a safety net stronger than either person ever imagined.

This is our charge in making our families everything they can be. This is the way to treat marriage as a covenant. This is the road to embracing family as a source of strength and clarity.

The same kind of clarity and personal power that flowed to James and Ellen can flow to siblings who overcome rivalry or more intense discord by getting to the bottom of what events and dynamics have fed it. The same benefits can flow to sons and daughters and mothers and fathers who unearth the answers as to *why* they have had difficulty loving one another more perfectly. The same benefits can even flow to a bereaved father who loses a child and finds, in his loss, the capacity to love more deeply than he ever imagined possible.

Robert Pirsig speaks to his own immeasurable experience of this kind in his book *Zen and the Art of Motorcycle Maintenance.* Pirsig's son, Chris, who figures so prominently in Pirsig's book, was murdered. In trying to come to terms with his son's death, Pirsig discovered another way to see life. He realized that he missed a lot more about his son than his physical presence, he missed his larger pattern. This pattern, like the so-called "coincidences" in the Universe, tied Pirsig and his son together in ways that were beyond human understanding.

❧

Some time later it became clearer that these thoughts were something very close to statements found in many "primitive" cultures. If you take that part of the pattern that is not the flesh and bones of Chris and call it the "spirit" of Chris or the "ghost" of Chris, then you can say without further translation that the spirit or ghost of Chris is looking for a new body to enter. When we hear accounts of "primitives" talking this way, we dismiss them as superstition because we interpret ghost or spirit as some sort of material ectoplasm, when in fact they may not mean any such thing at all.

In any event, it was not many months later that my wife conceived, unexpectedly. After careful discussion we decided it was not something that should continue. I'm in my fifties. I didn't want to go through any more child-raising experiences. I'd seen enough. So we came to our conclusion and made the necessary medical appointment.

Then something very strange happened. I'll never forget it. As we went over the whole decision in detail one last time, there was a kind of dissociation, as though my wife started to recede while we sat there talking. We were looking at each other, talking normally, but it was like those photographs of a rocket just after launching where you see two stages start to separate from each other in space. You think you're together and then suddenly you see that you're not together anymore.

I said, "Wait. Stop. Something's wrong." What it was, was unknown, but it was intense and I didn't want it to continue. It was a really frighten-

ing thing, which has since become clearer. It was the larger pattern of Chris, making itself known at last. We reversed our decision, and now realize what a catastrophe it would have been for us if we hadn't.

✎

Family bonds survive even the tragic death of a son. They remain as bread crumbs for us to find the way forward so long as we are willing to keep our eyes open for them and not drown in our own sorrow.

Even when we struggle within our families, even when we feel alone in them, we should remind ourselves that we have pens in our hands with which to "write" successful, healing chapters of our evolving family histories. Very often, we just need to "read" the chapters that have come before those we are living right now and understand them.

We know that the best efforts of people won't always heal the relationships on which they focus them. Some marriages end. Some parents remain unwilling or unable to show anything close to love. A brother or sister may become completely estranged from the family, and no attempt at reconciliation seems to have any hope of changing that reality.

Yet please understand this: putting forth such efforts

is essential. Sometimes athletes work for years and never win a title; that doesn't mean that all the work they put in was useless.

The search for a solid foundation in family is part of every person's journey to find his or her true path—his or her truth—because our families are encoded in our bio-chemical DNA, in our psychological DNA, and in God's plan for us. To move decisively forward in the direction God intended us to, to be ready for the moment when we each have the chance to bring ourselves most completely to this life we are living, we must first be willing to understand the lives of our families.

What Do I Know Without Having to Think So Much about It?

It is remarkable how many of the situations that caused me the most pain in life could have been avoided, and how many of the richest aspects of my life could have been embraced sooner had I just listened to my instincts. See, it wasn't a lack of common sense that made me resist the friendship of obviously good and decent people, or hold on to material possessions when I could ill afford them, or wait too long to devote myself to speaking about political issues and faith. It's that I wasn't able to *use* the common sense I did have.

I've learned that inside each of us is a kind of reflex arc that receives a myriad of information from our environment and accesses what we know about ourselves, including our life history and dreams for the future. This arc then does a lightning-fast calculation to assess any situation at hand. It's called common sense, and it's a true gift from God.

Here are a few examples of how common sense can manifest itself in everyday life:

- We unconsciously "tap into" the tone of someone's voice;
- We know whether a person looks directly at us or away from us when speaking or reacting to something;
- We notice whether someone asks a meaningful question about a concern we've raised or instead quickly changes the topic;
- We watch whether people who meet a new buddy of ours seem to gravitate toward him or keep their distance from him;
- We notice whether we feel comfortable about the clothes we try on in a store or instead have the sense we are overspending;
- We either feel excited and confident driving to

meet someone new for a date or feel like we're driving straight into trouble;

- We assess whether we are truly in love to the core of our beings or whether we are simply convincing ourselves to not dwell on qualities in a romantic partner that will irk us in six months or a year from now.

The list goes on and on, but the trouble is that while these gut feelings are often very accurate, we may barely register them. Worse, we may acknowledge them but then second-guess and quickly bury them.

There is a cultural myth that going over and over and over something in one's mind is the best way to get to the truth about it. But that isn't really the case. Very often our first impressions are the ones that turn out to be right, but we doubt them or fear them or argue against them, either in order to pretend we are safe or to justify some form of temporary pleasure.

In my heart of hearts, I *knew* when someone was just hanging around with me so that we could go looking for cocaine together, but I wasn't willing to hold that thought and focus on it because I *wanted* to get high.

I *knew* in my heart when I was dating a woman because she looked pretty and because she wouldn't try to go deeper than the surface of any discussion with me, but I couldn't bear to admit to myself that I was using the relationship as a shield against real intimacy.

I *knew* in my heart that the one-liners and pranks that made up a lot of my work as a DJ weren't anything close to the contribution I needed to make in this world, but I couldn't find the courage and faith to actually pursue work I would find more meaningful.

I *knew* in my heart that I was using the emblem on my Mercedes like a force field to protect me from anyone who might judge me a failure (which is what I felt like inside), yet I drove that car every day and even took pride in the envious glances that came my way.

I *knew* that Pat Gray was my true friend and had answers I needed in order to save my life, but I couldn't reach for that life preserver for years and years, even when I nearly drowned.

I *knew* that every hour I traded time with my kids for time for a bottle of Jack, I was cheating them and myself, but I drained plenty of bottles anyway.

I *knew* that every time I heard someone mention AA I was supposed to be going to those meetings, but I didn't go until alcohol nearly destroyed me.

I *knew* for years and years that losing my mother to suicide when I was thirteen had scarred me and led me to run away from truths that I ultimately needed to face, but I didn't sit down with a psychiatrist for decades.

I *knew* that my relationship with my father had to be rooted in losses he had suffered much earlier in his own life. But I waited until just a few years ago to learn what I needed to know about him to heal our relationship.

I *knew* that fantasizing about driving my car into a bridge abutment meant that I was deeply depressed, but I never once drove to an emergency room to tell anybody I needed help. If I had, I could have saved myself a lot of time and a whole bunch of trouble.

I *knew* in my heart that Tania was someone I felt drawn to from the moment I first met her. But I didn't *act* on that intuition—not even when she appeared again at the event I was hosting. I had to see her a third time to say more than a few words to her.

As before, this list goes on and on but you see the common theme—my common sense didn't fail me, I failed it. More important to ask is what about these situations alerted my gut before my brain? Take meeting Tania, for instance. How did I know so quickly that she was a woman I should be reaching out to?

I now believe that it was a myriad of variables that were instantly processed in my brain and nervous system, my mind and soul. They probably included the tone of her voice, the fact that she had instantly made eye contact with me when she introduced herself, and the fact that she was graceful in losing the raffle she entered. And, oh yeah, she was immensely beautiful as well.

I can't know all the variables. That's the point. I can't know all of them because they were being absorbed and assessed at lightning speed and mingling with my entire life history up until that very moment.

Even today, after thirteen years of marriage, knowing everything I know about my wife, I *still* can't solve the riddle of why I felt so comfortable walking right up to her the night I was going to end my sobriety. But, I swear to you, as I walked over to her table in that restaurant I felt like I was walking into my own home.

When I asked Tania to marry me I felt no anxiety. None. Zero. I don't know why. I don't know why, even after she turned me down, that I believed we would still end up being husband and wife one day.

I'm okay with not being able to solve the riddle of our connection. It's not a science. It's an art. It doesn't translate into a formula. Sure, you can see the notes on the page of a symphony by Beethoven, but that doesn't mean a reproduction will maintain its original power. Michelangelo could explain to you in great detail how he painted the ceiling of the Sistine Chapel, but that doesn't mean you'd be able to do it yourself.

Think about this another way. When people go to an animal shelter they often walk by several cages of animals before they stop and say, "That's the one. Can I hold *that* one?" Why?

Think about when you met your best friend in the world. You may have met that person in kindergarten or high school or college or five years ago or at your last job. But you did not select them by administering a personality test or by interviewing a dozen of the people who knew them well or by conducting a polygraph. It sounds ridiculous to even think about doing any of that, right? Of course—because you already trusted your gut, acted on it, and reaped the benefits.

My point is not to compare the selection of your best friend or soul mate to a poodle—but it's important to realize that we do many important things in our lives by trusting our gut. You cannot throw logic away, of course—it's imperative that we use the brains God gave us to help make smart judgments. But your brain and gut must be used in conjunction with each other.

Take the example I gave earlier about a dog barking when it senses danger, while humans sit there and rationalize. A dog relies *only* on its gut—something that sooner or later will result in it making terribly inaccurate judgments. A human, on the other hand, can combine their gut with their brain. Is the washing machine in the basement going and that's what caused the banging sound down there? If so, your dog would bark at the sound, while you'd dismiss it.

Think about the relationship that ended most painfully for you, one that ended because you learned the person wasn't reliable or wasn't considerate or wasn't truthful. Looking back, didn't you *know* something was amiss when you met that person? Maybe it was that they talked about someone negatively, and it struck you as kind of odd, but you let it go for some reason. Or maybe it was that they changed the time of a meeting twice without really inquiring if the changes were going to be a problem for you. Or maybe it was that you never heard them talk about their family, ever, until *you* asked about them. Whatever it was, you *knew* something wasn't quite right. You knew it in your gut and your brain (eventually) processed it.

Think about a time when you disappointed someone in your life and wished you could have taken it all back. Maybe you made a hurtful comment about that person and you *knew* as the words were coming out of your mouth that you were about to injure your relationship with them.

Maybe you made a bad choice at work that landed you in a gray ethical area and got you in deep trouble with your employer and you *knew*, even as you were taking steps in the wrong direction, away from your core principles, that it *was* the wrong direction.

Maybe you didn't show up at an event in a friend's life when you *knew*, despite all your rationalizing, that it was something your friend was counting on you to attend, and your absence fractured the relationship.

You *knew*. You knew in your heart of hearts. You knew in your gut. You knew in a way that you could never explain to anyone else other than that you just plain *did*.

That's common sense.

Over time, I've developed something that reminds me of what Keith already shared with you regarding a key element of his psychiatry training. He calls it the *third ear*—the ability to listen to himself while he listens to patients. I don't do it with patients because (fortunately, for society) I don't have any, but I do it in meetings and while I'm reading and while I'm talking to my kids and my wife and while I'm driving and while I'm doing my show. I do it dozens of times every day. I call it checking my gut or checking in with God, which amounts to the same thing. Because He gave me this gift, just like He gave it to you.

I literally try to focus on what I am *feeling* when I am introduced to someone new, or when I am called upon to make a critical decision or take a significant risk. It might sound odd, but if I can get quiet and focused enough, I can almost always detect what my gut is telling me.

Sometimes I'll be introduced to someone and get a "bad" feeling that the person isn't trustworthy, even though everyone has vouched for them. Sometimes I'll notice that I'm *trying* to be as positive as everyone else in the room about an idea, when the truth is that I am really having serious reservations about it. Sometimes I'll notice that I'm yielding ground on a project I supported, because a partner of mine is voicing so many doubts about it, when, deep inside, I *really* still believe we ought to move forward with it. Sometimes I'll get the impression—just by catching an instant of eye contact between two people in my office—that I need to help them resolve a problem they haven't felt okay coming to me about. So I'll go to them.

I used to dismiss feelings when they came to me "out of the blue." Now I see my gut feelings *as another kind of data*. Additional data that can help me make my decisions. You can't just walk through life reacting to every whim. You have to use reason, logic, and a careful consideration of the situation as well. But I've found that, over and over again, when I've ignored my gut I have been ignoring the most important information of all.

Now, I respect the radar God gave me as a gift. And it's not unique to me; we all have it.

I wouldn't feel foolish at all anymore if I were to say to

Tania, "You know something, I'd better stay up later tonight to go over things one more time. I thought I heard something in so-and-so's voice today that told me we're not quite prepared for the event tomorrow." Or, "When you asked me whether I'd be home this whole weekend or had any meetings, you sounded a little stressed, like you're worried about something. I could be wrong. I'm really not sure. But if I'm right, I'm here to listen." Or, "There's just something that bugs me about the contractor who just left here. I can't quite put my finger on it, but I think I'm going to go with the first one who came by. I just feel more comfortable."

Gut feelings don't always arrive on schedule. For example, sometimes I will have done all the thinking I can about a project and decided on a creative direction my team should take. We'll go down the road a piece and I'll crash—*smack*—right into my common sense. I'll *feel* that we made the wrong decision back, say three weeks earlier. I'll get just a quick glimpse of that fork in the road where we chose the wrong path. I might feel badly, of course, that we wasted time going in the wrong direction, but you can't achieve your best unless you are fully behind what you're doing. Making changes before you go down a road that you ultimately won't be proud of is always a good idea. Scrapping a journey because you have veered down the wrong path isn't wasting *anything*. It's part of the process of getting onto the right track. And when your gut tells you to do that, you should try to resist feeling like you've lost anything, because you're actually *finding* your way.

Think about it like this: It's cold and raining and you're stuck in a forest trying to get to a cottage where there's food and shelter and a warm bed. You've been walking a long time. You think you should head due east, so you walk in that direction for about fifteen minutes and then you realize, "No, this is wrong." So you readjust. It happens another half a dozen times before you finally see the cottage up ahead.

You have essentially zigzagged your way through the forest to the front door. You could certainly mourn every step that you "wasted," but that would be a colossal waste of energy. And it wouldn't even be true to the nature of the journey because reaching goals in life is very often all about zigzagging toward them. It's the way our souls *work*. To grieve that would be like grieving the sweat on your body during a marathon, or grieving every hill you encounter. If you want to run, you're going to sweat and you're going to face steep inclines. If you want to pursue goals in the world and listen to your heart and really get to where you should be going, then some of the time you will zigzag there. You have to. You're supposed to.

This hints at the remarkable synergy between common sense and faith. It is one thing to register in your gut what the right thing is, but it is quite another to do that thing and stick with it, even when you encounter pain or exhaustion or the anger of those who want you to get in line and stay there.

Combine common sense and faith, and you are a force—whether in your family or your company or your community or your country. You sense the direction you must head. You are willing to believe that your journey is an inspired one that you are meant to take. And you are willing to sacrifice to get there.

I have needed to harness this power the most when doing something that goes against common wisdom— and I suspect the same has been, or will be, true for you. The usual and accepted way of seeing things and doing things—*convention*—can be an extremely powerful force to overcome. When your instincts run counter to common wisdom, then doing God's work requires patience and compassion and courage and one other essential quality that really deserves a book of its own: endurance.

I think you'll notice something very interesting when

you begin to respect your common sense and combine it with faith. You won't scare easily. You won't doubt your ability to achieve what you want to achieve in this life because you won't doubt that God is not only *by* your side, but *in*side you. And trust me, that will be more than enough to get you through to a better place, and even bring other people along for the ride.

The Seventh Wonder: Common Sense

*I*f we have God-given common sense in our souls, then what prevents us from using it? How can we be intelligent about so many things in life and experienced in so many ways, yet still make mistakes that cost us so much?

Thinking about one of my patients, a thirty-seven-year-old single woman I'll call Maggie, can help us answer those questions. I've written about her before in my book *Living the Truth*, but her story is worth repeating here because of how illustrative it is of this particular wonder.

Maggie came to see me after being fired as an executive at a manufacturing company barely a year after she started. She'd never had anything but glowing reviews from bosses at other companies and she said she felt "humiliated." Looking for a new position with a black mark on her résumé, she said, was keeping her up at night and preventing her from concentrating during the day. Her migraines, which she hadn't had since she was a teenager, were back.

"It would be one thing if I'd hated this woman from day one," Maggie said of her boss, Elizabeth. "But I liked her. I trusted her. And she totally used me." She paused. "I thought I knew people. I was really stupid."

Maggie looked genuinely hurt. "How did she 'use' you?" I asked.

"I left a really, really good job at my last company because she recruited me. She was always telling me at trade shows how talented I was and how she'd love to work with me. Then she made me an offer. I took it. I poured my whole heart into her company. I definitely put in more time than I ever had before—eighty, ninety hours a week, traveling to Europe and China and everywhere else. It was nonstop for thirteen months. And then all of a sudden she's like, 'This isn't working out.'"

"Did she say why?"

"Ridiculous stuff," Maggie said. "My attitude. Shipping glitches, which I had zero control over." She paused. "From what I hear, this is just Elizabeth's thing. It happened to two other people who had the job before me. One lasted a year; the other a year and a half. She gets nervous someone will take over or something."

"When did you find out about these other people?" I asked.

"People at the company told me before I signed on," she said. "I should have known this was going to end badly. I *did* know. I just wanted to think it would be different with me. I convinced myself of it."

"How?"

"Well, Elizabeth said the other women acted as if landing the job meant they didn't have to be hands-on anymore—as if they could just sit back and delegate. And I pride myself on never asking anyone who works with me to do more than I do. Plus, I had this connection with her. Or I thought I did."

"What sort of connection was that?" I asked.

"She seemed to want to help me get to the next level," Maggie said. "I've never worked directly for a woman before. I've always thought it would be the best situation for me." She sighed. "Dumb."

"Not dumb," I assured her. "You wanted a mentor."

She shrugged. "I've just never felt completely comfortable with the men I've worked for. Maybe it's the glass-ceiling thing. Or maybe it's me. I don't know. It's been hard for me to trust men."

"Why is that?"

"Because my dad was an ass."

That sounded pretty straightforward. "How so?"

"The usual way," she said. "He cheated on my mother."

"Did they divorce?"

"When I was eleven. But that was after putting my mother through hell for years."

"You knew about your dad's infidelity?" I asked.

"My mother and I don't keep secrets from each other."

"She told you?"

"I found out about it the minute she did. I remember her screaming at him that he couldn't come to my seventh birthday party because she'd found a girl's number in his pocket." She smiled. "Sandra."

"Why are you smiling?" Keith asked.

She shrugged. "I just think it's funny I never forgot her name. The others are a blur."

The fact that Maggie had never forgotten that name wasn't funny at all, of course. "You're not angry about what happened?" I asked.

Her smile disappeared. "At him, nobody else. I hardly speak to him."

I understood Maggie's anger. I knew that at seven years old, Maggie would have been attached to her father in complex ways, including (at least according to Sigmund Freud) unconscious fantasies about becoming the sole focus of her father's affections, in place of her mother. The fact that she had had to acknowledge that her father was apparently passionate about a third woman—a stranger—would have made her feel jealous and enraged.

But Maggie's words told me more than that. My "third ear" registered that she seemed intent on him knowing that she was angry at "only" her father. And that didn't seem to make sense. It made me feel as though she were holding up a shield to keep herself—and him—from the truth. After all, two people had hurt Maggie: Her father had done it by being careless and callous enough to disclose his sexual indiscretions. Her mother had done it by sharing highly charged information with her when she was clearly incapable of understanding it. From the moment Maggie's mother learned of her husband's infidelity, she had apparently used Maggie as a pawn to get back at him, barring him from showing up at their daughter's seventh birthday party.

But Maggie couldn't have allowed herself to feel angry with both her parents. That would have made her feel too alone. Knowing that her father could leave for another woman, she would have needed to believe that

someone would protect and love her forever. She turned
to her mother, even though it didn't sound to me like her
mother had earned her confidence.

"You're very close with your mom?" I asked Maggie.

"She's my best friend," Maggie said. "We've been
through everything together."

In fact, I learned that Maggie had signed on with
her mother for war after war. There were her father's repeated infidelities. There was her parents' divorce. Then
there were the half dozen or so tumultuous romances her
mother suffered through, each of them ending with the
discovery that the boyfriend was either married or ad-
dicted to drugs or seeing other women.

In turn, Maggie's mom had come to her daughter's
defense each time Maggie chose a man "unworthy" of her
trust or affection. And that happened a lot. Even at work,
her male bosses always seemed to be egotists, predators,
or frauds. And her mother was always there, a shoulder to
cry on.

I knew that challenging Maggie's belief that her
mother was beyond reproach would connect her with
early and intense feelings of fear and betrayal. I would be
asking her to feel all the pain she would have felt at seven
had she admitted to herself that neither her father nor her
mother was able to put her first, that she wasn't *that* well
loved by anyone. To a child, that would have felt like the

whole world could fall apart at any time; that her very survival was in question. And part of Maggie was still that child.

I also knew, however, that Maggie had come to therapy after her *female* employer disappointed her. And she had come to *me*—a man—for help. That told me that she might be ready to abandon the gender stereotypes and family myths that were keeping her from seeing the true nature of her predicament as a child—and moving beyond it.

"Why wasn't your mother more careful to keep what she found out about your father to herself?" I asked Maggie during their next session.

She squinted at me in disbelief. "You're joking, right?"

"Not at all."

She stood up. "This is ridiculous. How can you be taking his side?"

"I'm not," I replied. "I'm taking yours."

She started toward the door.

I wanted to make sure that Maggie understood I believed that her leaving would be a form of denial. "You can't avoid the truth forever," I said.

She turned back to face me. "It was her job to cover for him?" she seethed.

"That's not what I'm saying," I said gently. I motioned toward Maggie's seat, hoping she'd take it again.

She didn't move.

"It was her job to protect your relationship with him, even if he violated theirs," I said.

"There was nothing to protect."

"Maybe not," I allowed. I paused. "Do you remember anything about your dad from when you were, say, five or six?"

"Nothing good," she said.

I nodded, but stayed silent. Several seconds passed.

"What are you getting at?" Maggie asked. "I mean, he took me to the park and stuff. What father doesn't? But when it came to—"

Plenty of fathers don't. "What sort of park?"

"A *park*. I don't know. It wasn't anything special. It had this really high slide and swings and rides, or whatever."

"What did you like to do there?"

That was a simple question, but it opened up memories that Maggie had shut down in order to maintain a version of her life story that was partly fiction: that her father was the enemy and her mother was her only ally.

She rolled her eyes. "I don't know why this matters."

"Tell me anyhow."

She sighed. "The slide, okay? You went up a ladder that must have had about twenty steps and . . ." She stopped herself. "What does this have to do with . . . ?"

Almost any father who has raised a daughter, as both Glenn and I have, can picture her at the top of a slide like the one Maggie had described—half excited, half petrified.

"Did he tell you you'd be all right sliding down?" I asked Maggie. "Did he wait for you at the bottom?"

She just looked over at me. Her eyes filled with tears. She wiped them, then shook her head. "Why are you doing this?"

I pressed forward. "What else did you two do together?"

A tear rolled down Maggie's cheek. "He drove me to school every day."

"Did you like that?"

Another tear. "Stop," Maggie said. She finally sat down.

I did stop, but Maggie's tears didn't—for half a minute, maybe more.

During our next meeting, I pressed Maggie to recall more of the good times she had had with her father. I also urged her to more realistically evaluate her mother's behavior. "Did you think your mom had bad luck choosing men?" I asked. "Or bad judgment."

"How was she supposed to know if some guy was a loser?"

"Guy after guy?"

"She's supposed to be a mind reader?"

"No, just a mother. And that means being careful who she includes in her daughter's life."

Maggie looked me straight in the eye, as if deciding whether she could really trust me. "I guess I would have been more careful if I were her," she said finally, just above a whisper.

It didn't take more than a few hours for Maggie to make the connection between her mother having selected one damaged man after another and her own habit of doing the same. Not only was she deprived of the love of her father from a young age, but she never learned how to include a worthy man in her life.

I remembered Maggie telling me her logic for thinking that a female employer would be the right fit for her. *I've just never felt completely comfortable with the men I've worked for.*

Is that really any wonder? Maggie had seen her father unmasked as a philanderer and then portrayed as a scoundrel. She had witnessed the predictable results of her mother continuing to favor broken, unreliable men. So Maggie had almost no chance of drawing any conclusion other than that *all* men were untrustworthy, even her male employers. Why would she have ever looked to one of them for nurturance or mentoring?

Carl Jung eloquently explained the way that the unexamined chapters of our life stories end up taking control of our decision making and scrambling the inner voice of truth inside us—the voice of God:

That which we do not bring to consciousness appears in our lives as fate.

Having the courage and faith to bring truth into consciousness allows you to access your God-given common sense.

I didn't even have to ask Maggie the question most directly related to her having misjudged the character of the woman who hired her away from her prior job, encouraged her to work ninety hours a week, then summarily fired her, apparently for no good reason. Maggie asked that question herself. "You know, I never even considered believing that Elizabeth had fired two other people for no reason. Do you think," she wondered aloud, "that wanting to see my mother as perfect meant I couldn't really see Elizabeth for who she was?"

Exactly. Maggie *knew* when she heard about Elizabeth's former, short-lived employees that leaving a good-paying job to work with her was a big risk. She probably could have gotten contact information for the other women who had held the position she ended up taking, reached out to them, and come to a reasoned decision about whether they really seemed like the slouches Elizabeth described. She probably could have used her contacts in the industry to inquire with executives at other companies what they thought of Elizabeth. But she overrode her concerns in order to perpetuate the overvalued idea that an older, female role model would not lie to her or manipulate her. She didn't use her common sense because she wanted to remain comfortably swathed in a myth.

This is the self-defeating formula that leads people to invest their money with fraudulent advisers and money managers. Bernie Madoff, the infamous Ponzi scheme operator, for example, was generating annual returns year after year that made many of those who invested with him wonder at a gut level whether his performance was too good to be true. But they didn't withdraw their money from his funds because they were clinging to myths, including the intoxicating idea that they were smart enough or well enough connected to have found a financial guru who could beat the system again and again and again. And even if that drug wasn't potent enough to keep them invested, there was the specter of all the pain they would have to experience if they did cash out and everyone else continued to profit year after year.

This is the self-defeating formula that leads people to begin and maintain romantic relationships with manipulative partners who they *know* at some level are telling them everything they want to hear while violating their trust over and over again. But it feels *good*, at another level, to *hear* those things, so they don't investigate those partners too deeply, until it's too late.

This is the self-defeating formula that leads people to stay wedded to alcohol or drugs when they *know* they are sowing the seeds of their own destruction. But it *feels* good to put some distance between our conscious thoughts and our underlying, unresolved issues, so they pour that next drink or smoke that next joint anyway.

This is the self-defeating formula that leads people to allow thieves and even killers into their lives, despite *gut feelings* that danger looms, because it feels *good* to be kind and openhearted and because they don't want to surrender the comforting illusion that the world is safe and predictable and that they will never be called upon to face down a thug or a killer.

This is also the self-defeating formula that leads people to agree with ideas that they *know* are illogical. During the Internet stock bubble of the 1990s, when companies went public with massive debts and little or no earnings, many millions of Americans agreed publicly with the idea that it was no longer reasonable to value companies based on earnings. Only the "story" of the company really mattered, because the Internet was such a rocket ship that everyone needed to get aboard as soon as possible. Wow, that felt *good* to think about. All that wealth being created out of thin air. Privately, of course, those same Americans were shaking their heads over dinner, saying things like "This can't go on forever; it's insanity." But that felt *bad* to think about, so they bought even more of those stocks the next morning. And the next. And the next. And when the stocks crashed and burned, the same Americans were telling the truth when they said, "We knew that was coming. I don't know why we didn't sell when we could have."

It is the self-defeating formula that leads people to support politicians who promise them that they can own homes without the income to support them, send their kids to overcrowded, drug-riddled schools and still keep them safe and get them educated, and receive all manner of free government services by shifting the cost of those giveaways to future generations who will somehow have the magical power to make it all come out in the wash. Because even with common sense raining a little bit on the parade, believing those myths feels *good*. And focusing on all the hard work that has to be done in order to actually create financial strength in one's personal life or one's nation feels *bad*.

But this is also the self-defeating formula that leads

people to dismiss great opportunities that they know deep in their hearts feel *right* even when conventional wisdom says they are *wrong*. It keeps people in jobs that pay more but give them less satisfaction. It keeps them quiet when they have the seeds of great ideas inside them but worry they will be dismissed or laughed at. It keeps them pretending to be satisfied in their marriages when they need to say they aren't and get to work healing what needs healing. It keeps them from starting businesses and novels and charities and youth groups and political campaigns and friendships that keep tugging at them for attention. It keeps them from saying yes to the voice of God inside them.

It isn't easy. I know that. Even well into my psychiatry training, I had an experience that showed me just how hard it is to honor what you feel inside about the truth of a particular situation.

I was called by my adviser, the late and revered Boston psychiatrist Ted Nadelson, M.D., to evaluate a man I'll call Tom. Tom, forty-two years old, had arrived in the emergency room and it seemed that both he and the staff needed support at the same time. See, this man's story was so painful that it had brought a few of the nurses and the ER doctor to tears.

When I first saw Tom, I was taken aback by the scratches all over his face and body and the deep laceration across his forehead. But even those dramatic injuries paled in comparison to what he described having gone through over the prior forty-eight hours.

In tears, Tom told me that he had been driving with his wife and daughters, ages seven and nine, in New Hampshire, going north on Interstate 95, when another vehicle crossed the median and hit them head-on. Tom's airbag had deployed, but his pickup truck had no passenger airbag, and his little girls had not been wearing seat belts in the back of the crew cab. His wife and both daughters had died instantly. Tom had lingered by the side of the highway until they were pronounced dead at the scene, then had disappeared into the woods and literally walked for two days until he reached the medical center.

"I came here because this is where my girls . . . They were born here," Tom wept. "And I as much as killed them. Tracy told me to get rid of that truck and get something safer. And I should have had those kids in their seat belts." He began to rock back and forth in such agony that a nurse literally jogged to his bed with another dose of Valium. He was shaking so much that he poured the water all over himself and barely got the pill down.

"Let me ask you one question," I said.

Tom nodded, looked me in the eyes for an instant, but then dropped his gaze.

"Did your wife and daughters know you loved them when you got into that car?" I went on.

Tom took a deep breath and let it out. He nodded.

"Then they knew it when they left this life. I want you to focus on that. Just that, for now. Okay?"

Tom looked up at the ceiling, seemingly searching for something. He began to sob. "Okay, Doc," he said. "Okay, I'm gonna try that. Thank you. You're a kind man. I don't deserve anyone's kindness." He closed his eyes.

The Valium was, mercifully, starting to take effect.

After writing up Tom's clinical history, I went to see Ted Nadelson.

Dr. Nadelson was a big man, with silver hair and pale blue eyes and two hearing aids that I always thought meant that he had listened to so many stories that he'd worn his ears out. "Tough case," Nadelson said, from behind his old oak desk. "I heard about it from the ER director. He's rattled, and he doesn't rattle easily. You must be feeling it, too. Tell me."

I thought about agreeing that Tom's story was one of the worst I had ever heard. I thought about paying lip service to the idea that I was a little shaken up by it, because I was worried that actually acknowledging and admitting what I was really feeling would make me look peculiar or naïve or insensitive in front of my mentor. I didn't want to go against the common wisdom at the medical center and be *judged* as having no empathy. But I was in a psychiatry training program based on acknowledging one's own truth and using it to help other people find theirs. So

I just decided to say what I really felt. "I felt nothing," I said. "He told me all about losing his family and how he was to blame and how he walked two days to this hospital where his daughters were born, and I felt nothing."

Nadelson looked at me askance. "Did you lose anyone you loved in a car crash? I'm just fishing, I know. But . . ."

I shook my head.

"You didn't lose a sibling as a kid, did you?"

"No, and . . ." I started, then stopped short, worried that my next thought wasn't worth adding.

Nadelson smiled. "C'mon, let's have it."

"Okay, I'm not saying it means anything, all right?"

Nadelson stayed silent.

"But when I was talking to Tom," I said, "I told him I had a question for him, and he looked me in the eyes for a second, then looked down." I literally chuckled at the thought that I was actually making so much of this gut feeling. "I got the sense that he was looking at my loafers, like squinting at them, in order to see what kind they were." This was the part that seemed the most outlandish: "I felt like he envied them."

Nadelson glanced over the desk at my loafers. "They new?"

"Yup."

"Very nice. Very fancy."

"Half what you pay me for a week."

Nadelson smiled and nodded. "And you're think-ing why would a man who has just lost his wife and two daughters care what sort of loafers you're wearing. That about right?"

"Pretty much," I said.

"I guess you'd better do two things," Nadelson said.

I prepared for advice on how to soften my heart.

"First, check with the New Hampshire State Police to see whether they've responded to any traffic fatalities in the last three days. And then check the hospital records here to see if they include the patient's wife delivering two children here."

"Really?"

"Keith, if you learn nothing else from me," Nadelson said, "learn to trust your gut enough to never, ever dis-miss it. Sometimes you'll have to figure out why you were feeling the way you were, and the answer may be very different from what you initially guessed. But you'll never find out there was *no* reason for feeling that way."

I did what Nadelson had suggested. I learned there had been no traffic fatality on Interstate 95 in New Hamp-shire, nor in bordering Massachusetts for months. The hospital had no record of any patient with Tom's wife's name, nor any record of the birth of babies with his daughters' names.

When I reviewed the Emergency Room chart, it was

remarkable how much Valium Tom had received and how his head pain had intensified so that it required repeated doses of Vicodin, a narcotic pain reliever.

Tom was, in fact, a substance abuser who had come to the emergency room to get as high as possible. He was so determined to do so that (as he later admitted) he had scratched himself with a stick and then struck his forehead with a brick to bruise it and cut it open.

Yet even with all his subterfuge and all his determination, Tom's single envious glance down at my loafers ultimately gave him away. With help from Ted Nadelson, I ultimately felt neither too afraid nor too embarrassed nor too arrogant to say what I really felt and act on it. I didn't defeat my own common sense, I embraced it.

Well, guess what? You don't have to defeat your common sense, either. You can begin honoring your gut feelings today by following these three steps:

STEP ONE:

Practice Listening to Your Gut as You Are Listening to People's Words or Reading the Newspaper or Watching Television or Perusing the Web Throughout the Day

In order to do this, you need to listen for inner voices inside you. They may speak at a whisper, but they do speak.

If you are very attentive to them you will not just tap into a nondescript sense of uneasiness or doubt or excitement; you will hear actual words in your head. They might be general, like "I don't think I quite believe that." But they might also be quite specific, like "If you really are so attentive to detail as a landscaper, why does your truck have two missing hubcaps and a rusted dent in it?"

Walk around your office or your house or down the street and give yourself the chance to commune with your knee-jerk impressions of things. If you look at someone's desk, think about what it's making you feel inside about that person. If you receive a letter, read it and focus on the feelings it evokes in you. When you get a call, listen to the conversation at the same time as you monitor the unspoken thoughts and feelings that conversation brings up in you.

In *Intoxicated by My Illness*, Anatole Broyard, the late editor of the *New York Times Book Review*, wrote about his impressions of the hospitals and doctors he met as he began battling prostate cancer. They're instructive, because Broyard was able to note how he felt inside about what he saw around him. And he had the self-esteem and confidence to act on those immeasurable, inexplicable feelings.

When Broyard met one urologist, for example, he was immediately disenchanted with the way the doctor looked during a diagnostic procedure. And Broyard *acted on it* by choosing to not keep him as his physician:

❦

During surgical procedures, doctors wear a tight-fitting white cap, a sort of skullcap like one Alan Alda wears on M*A*S*H. To this my doctor had added what looked like a clear plastic shower cap, and the moment I saw him in these two caps, I turned irrevocably against him. He wore them absolutely without inflection or style, with none of the jauntiness that usually comes with long practice. Now, I think a doctor who has been around, he knows how to do these things. There was no attempt to mitigate the two caps. The first was like a condom stuck on his head. He didn't look good in it. He had a round face, and in the cap he looked confused and uncertain. He wore it like an American in France who affects a beret without understanding how to shape or cock it. To my eyes this doctor simply didn't have the charisma to overcome or assimilate those caps, and this completed my disaffection.

I want to point out that this man was in all likelihood an able, even a talented, doctor. Certainly, I'm no judge of his medical competence, nor do I mean to criticize it. What turned me against him was what I saw as a lack of style or magic. I realized I wanted my doctor to have magic as well as medical ability. It was like having a lucky doctor. I've described all this—a patient's madness—to show how irrational such transactions are, how far removed from objectivity. . . . Still, this does not necessarily mean I was wrong to want to change doctors: I was simply listening to my unconscious telling me what I needed.

∞

Broyard was listening through more than just his ears, and he acted on what he heard. Would it not be foolhardy to go forward and be operated on by a surgeon who has inspired no confidence in you?

That sets the stage for the next two steps.

STEP TWO:

Practice Honoring Some of the Inner Voices
You Hear by Speaking Out Loud About
Them to at Least One Other Person

This can mean asking a simple question based on your instincts. If someone is describing an investment opportu-

nity that strikes you as overly optimistic, don't resist saying so and using the language of *gut feelings.*

"You know," you might say, "when you describe the
company as being bulletproof, I get this feeling that it all
sounds too good to be true. I don't mean to offend you,
but you've got to help me understand why I wouldn't just
stick with that feeling and pass on this opportunity."

Here are a few other examples:

"I would love to believe what you're saying about
never having felt this kind of passion for anyone else. Really. I would. But then I think about the fact that you're
fifty-two and you've been married a few times and you've
dated a lot, and I worry, 'Maybe he thinks he *has* to say
these things or maybe he says them automatically.' So, I
think we should take it a little slower. We have to *trust*
each other. I'll be able to see when you're that taken by
me; you won't have to say a word."

Or . . .

"I like that woman who came into our office to interview, but I didn't quite understand why she felt comfortable telling us about shopping for a new dress before
coming here. I mean, everything else sounded great, but
that made me wonder if she's looking for friends or a place
to work. I wonder if she'll be comfortable with authority.
What did you think?"

The next step is the hardest, but it can become a way
of life and a way to stay true to your path in life.

Act On Your Gut Feelings a Few Times, Without Fearing That You're Being Impulsive by Not Processing More "Data"

Say no to a date because your gut tells you it just doesn't feel like it will lead anywhere. Ask someone out on a date because your gut has been telling you that the two of you might form a special bond. Schedule time with someone who has been working on a project for you that you *feel* should be moving more quickly, and tell them so. Pull the plug on a project that has been sapping your energy and that you never really believed would succeed anyhow. Go on the Web and research the history of the ideas expressed by a political candidate you sense could be a great leader. Donate to that person's campaign or volunteer for that person if you continue to *feel* positive about the person after your research.

You were born with a barometer of truth inside you. You have the ability to process data faster than any computer ever created. Everything you have learned from books and all the *common wisdom* to which you have been exposed in life is no match for your God-given intuition.

You were born knowing that you deserve to be loved unconditionally, no matter what you have since learned to the contrary. You were born knowing that you deserve honesty from others, no matter what your experience has been to the contrary. You were born knowing that you have a right to defend yourself from harm, no matter what you might have surmised from having been bullied in the past. You were born knowing that you have the right to be represented by honest and decent and intelligent leaders who do what they promise they will do and never ask you to settle for subterfuge or embrace a myth. You were born knowing that you owe others your best—no less—and no matter how you may have stumbled in delivering that in the past. You were born knowing that you and others not only deserve to be happy but that you can promote their well-being.

You were born knowing that the truth always wins and that *You are the temple of God.*

Dare to communicate with your common sense. Dare to act upon it. It will never betray you.

Helping Others to Heal

There is another phenomenon in the emotional, intellectual, and psychological makeup of people that Glenn and I want to tap into with this book. We believe in a sort of kindling effect—the notion that people who come to see themselves and the world in a different way have a spirit that is contagious to others. We believe that your holding this book in your hands and absorbing what you absorb about the Seven Wonders can not only change your life, but also the lives of those with whom you interact.

Of course, that would be true without your mentioning this book at all. Because if you put the wonders to work in your existence, those around you will be emboldened simply by the example of your commitment to courage, faith, compassion, truth, friendship, family, and common sense.

We are all beacons. We not only attract to ourselves those with our own optimism or pessimism, our own self-love or self-hatred; we also broadcast our inner spiritual lives in a way that can hurt or heal others.

We hope you won't feel timid about actually speaking to others about any parts of this book that made sense to you or changed you or challenged you or even caused you concern. We want these ideas to enter the stream that flows inexplicably through the hearts and minds of human beings, no matter where they are or what their backgrounds may be.

This isn't about sales. Of course we're happy to sell books, but money is not the issue. This is about soul. This book is our best attempt to share what we know about how lives change for the better. We hope our children and their children can read it. We feel that good about it. Otherwise, we wouldn't feel comfortable asking you to read it, or think about it, or speak of it.

These are tough times. These are times when too many men and women are confused and adrift, needlessly

believing that they are empty and that there is no meaning to their lives or no way that they can ever be effective.
Nothing could be further from the truth. You may well
have known that before. You should surely know it now.
Help relieve their pain. Reach out to people to steady
them and enrich them and reflect back to them the light
that comes from God inside them.

You are the temple of God, we read in the Bible. And so
is your brother, and your sister, and your father, and your
mother, and your friend, and your adversary, and your
employee, and your employer, and that woman selling
you a suit of clothes, and that man asking you for a hand-
out on the street. Every single one of us has magic inside
us that can transform our lives and the lives of others. Try
not to be shy about your power. Try not to be embarrassed by it. Try not to run from it. Believe in it. Use it. It
is nothing less than your birthright. It gives you license—
agency, if you will—to fill your life and the lives around
you with wonder.

Leading with the Seven Wonders

How can it be that Mahatma Gandhi won independence for India from the British without taking up arms? How did he marry his force of will to that of an entire people in order to change the course of history?

The answer is that he showed courage in facing his adversaries, had faith that he was pursuing a just and righteous cause, sought the truth relentlessly, had compassion even for those whom he opposed, took confidence and comfort from his family and friends, and used his common sense. There were other ingredients to Gandhi's particular magic, no doubt, but the seven wonders were certainly alive in his thoughts and his deeds. Gandhi said:

❧

When I despair, I remember that all through history the ways of truth and love have always won. There have been tyrants, and murderers, and for a time they can seem invincible, but in the end they always fall. Think of it—always.

❧

How can it be that Martin Luther King, Jr., galvanized the spirit of millions of African Americans and inspired them to march for freedom? He was an incredible orator. He was a forceful presence. But he also embodied courage, faith, truth, and compassion; he loved his family, embraced his friends, and used his common sense. King said:

❧

Darkness cannot drive out darkness; only light can do that. Hate cannot drive out hate; only love can do that.

How can it be that George Washington could lead America to victory over the British, preside over the writing of the Constitution, be the unanimous choice of our Founding Fathers to serve as the first president of the United States, and then put his ego aside to surrender that office, lest he become royalty? He embodied courage, faith, truth, compassion, duty to family and friends, and a reliance on common sense. Washington said:

It will be found an unjust and unwise jealousy to deprive a man of his natural liberty upon the supposition he may abuse it.

How can it be that Samuel Adams was able to educate and motivate enough people to thirst for independence and put their lives on the line for it, then help etch the principles of our new nation into our history forever? He embodied courage, faith, truth, compassion, duty to family and friends, and a reliance on common sense. Adams said:

Let us awaken then, and evince a different spirit,—
a spirit that shall inspire the people with confidence
in themselves and in us,—a spirit that will encour-
age them to persevere in this glorious struggle, until
their rights and liberties shall be established on a
rock.

You can lead with the Seven Wonders, too. First, you must know yourself. You must use courage and faith to empty out the hard drive of your soul and then fill it with your truth. Because only from that solid foundation will you have enough compassion for others and enough confidence in your ideas and plans, to move people. You really will need the support of family and friends because nothing can replace those sources of warmth and honesty in your life. Without that support you can't have the kind of solid footing that allows you to walk worthy paths that inevitably course through darkness, and have others follow you, without ever losing hope. And you will need to be in touch with your common sense, lest you be drawn off course by comfortable, insufficient solutions to problems that require clear thinking, bold action, and a willingness to confront adversity.

The Seven Wonders are not a recipe for leadership or success; they are merely the raw ingredients. We don't know how God puts them together to create momentum and motivation and miracles that change families and communities and companies and countries, but we know He does. And that's okay with us. Because we don't have to know *how* it's done, we just have to know that it is. We just have to pray for it, witness it, believe it, and dedicate ourselves to being the vessels for it.

To continue your journey, please visit:
www.glennbeck.com/the7